THE MARKETING OF HISTORIC SITES, MUSEUMS, EXHIBITS & ARCHIVES

] ISBN #:   1-57440-056-8

TABLE OF CONTENTS

INTRODUCTION

This report looks closely at how history is presented and marketed by organizations such as history museums, libraries, historical societies, and historic sites and monuments, as well as by purveyors of archives, photographs, posters, and memorabilia.

The development, presentation, and marketing of history is one of our largest industries, encompassing huge swaths of tourism, entertainment, advertising, publishing, education, government, and arts and leisure. From the big money involved in history tourism, to the vast expenditures of institutions of higher education and museums, to the impact of heritage consulting in the advertising industry, to the dominance of history-oriented entertainment content on cable television, it's clear that history shapes much of our leisure time and work life. History is the favorite subject on best-seller lists and one of the hottest topics in cable television.

Despite this, attendance at major historic sites, monuments and museums has been falling in the United States. One reason is that Americans are less educated in history than they have been in the past, and, in general, attend fewer events than they once did. One of the most important questions for historic sites, collections, museums, societies and other purveyors of history is: How can we tap into the deep-seated need to recover and experience the past, while making sure this takes place away from the television screen or the movie-house? History museums and sites are not just competing with professional sports and situation comedies for the time and attention of the public, but with the many historical documentaries and movies offered through cable television and the internet. In recent years, it has become far more possible to experience history at home.

More so than other organizations in American life, history museums, and historical societies, archives, monuments, and sites have not taken advantage of the internet. They have underestimated its impact on travel and leisure decision-making, particularly among the largely upper and upper-middle income segments that tend to visit historic sites and museums. Moreover, they have not understood how the ubiquity of cable television, the internet and other new media forms, has transformed how Americans view history. The history "market" has never been more competitive, and just as live performance drama must make great efforts to compete with the plethora of new entertainment mediums, historic sites and museums must make similar or greater efforts to pull in visitors.

Perhaps the primary difference between the history market of 25 years ago and the history market today is that so much high quality material is available for free. Websites, blogs, newsgroups, documentaries and much more are available at the click of a mouse. Historic places must offer a level of experience that is significantly superior, or at least markedly different, from that offered on cable television and the internet. Yet historic sites and societies have lagged badly in exploiting these new mediums. The level of expectation has changed. Internet-savvy travelers expect better travel deals and expect new experiences in familiar places. Historic sites and monuments need to expand their web presence and offer new exhibits to keep themselves in the public mind.

As organized religion, political parties and national membership organizations have seen their influence wane in the America of the 21st century, history has the potential to re-awaken basic identities based on religion, ethnicity, geographic place, class, profession, and shared common experience. Through grassroots marketing, an expanded web presence, the formation of partnerships, and other tactics, America's historic sites are working to maintain and expand their grip on the nation's imagination, and travel and education budget.

Organizations that present and market history have to ask themselves: What is our place in the greater scheme of things? What are (and what can be) our ties to the local school system? To the adult education system? On the internet? To the travel industry?

The Vermont Historical Society used a grassroots approach to marshal its local area history resources, present them in novel ways, and ultimately win broad public recognition and corporate financial support. The key to the Society's success was innovative relationship-building among local partners such as schools and local historical societies, designed to capture the strengths of each party. Through aggressive and bold grassroots efforts, the Vermont Historical Society has been able to raise $7.5 million for a significant organizational face-lift, beating by more than $7 million its prior fundraising records. Although local activism and participation in local affairs is a hallmark of the Vermontian character, the local activist character lurks in all Americans, and the Vermont Historical Society shows how to coax it out.

Hook's Historical Drug Store and Pharmacy shows the enduring appeal of the 20th-century drug store and soda fountain on the American imagination, a memory exploited by other historic sites in this study. Hook's diversified into science education, exploiting an opening created by the slow down in local education spending nationwide. This slow down, though regrettable, creates many opportunities for organizations that steward and present historic legacies.

The Thomas Jefferson Foundation, whose major asset is Jefferson's former plantation, Monticello, demonstrates how a web of relationships can be developed by marketing all of the various and intricate facets of the Jeffersonian legacy.

At the other end of the history market, the scrappy Musee Conti Wax Museum of New Orleans shows how to bring a region's history to life in that most popular of sculpting mediums – wax. The Wax Museum has been particularly successful in hitting the corporate-travel and incentive-travel markets.

The Bostonian Society not only successfully projects Boston's Revolutionary War Heritage to its largely non-Bostonian visitor base, but also manages to capitalize on historic figures such as Ted Williams from a less lofty, but not less well-known, playing field. The Society has had particular success with digitizing its extensive photography collection, as have many public libraries. The Denver Public Library, for example, has had a great deal of success in presenting its digitized images of the American West to the broader public. Evansville Public Library, on the other hand, has focused more on an innovative approach to presenting local history through digital mediums.

The Dittrick Medical History Center, housed at Case Western Reserve University, has exploited a major new gift of a historic collection of contraceptive devices, to dramatically increase its web presence. The Museum has had particular success with aggressive cross-marketing with healthcare-oriented professional associations, hospitals and other museums in the medical arena.

The Band Museum, in Pine Bluff, Arkansas, and the Atari Virtual Museum, are mostly one-man efforts led by determined individuals who have a love of their subject matter. In both cases, the resulting history museums appealed mostly to important niche audiences that were underserved by existing cultural institutions.

The Belmont Mansion's grassroots marketing approach emphasizes public programming designed to bring in the patrons and sell them on return trips. Belmont has also benefited from a Tennessee state program to distribute press releases electronically, as well as from approaches to the bank travel market.

The Kansas State Historical Society, entrusted with the management of 16 state historic sites as well as the state archives, and offices for preservation and archeology, has recently completed a major $50,000 market research study that included focus groups, intercept surveys and telephone surveys.

The Computer History Museum relies heavily on a vast network of industry contacts to launch what has become one of the premier technology history sites in the country. Targeted marketing through an innovative website, frequent events and lectures, special programs for important niches, and close relations with a far-flung board of directors have been its keys to marketing success.

The Museum of American Financial History, based near Ground Zero in lower Manhattan, climbed back from the devastation of the 9/11 terrorist attacks and rebuilt its relationship with its patrons. In cooperation with 15 other museums in lower Manhattan, the Museum used Federal money specially earmarked for organizations victimized in the terror attacks, to develop a unique marketing campaign. The Museum also emphasizes the cultivation of ties with the press.

The Atlanta History Center, which recently purchased the Margaret Mitchell Site and Museum, has expanded the scope of its operations significantly in recent years. Unlike many historic attractions in recent years, the Atlanta History Center has experienced rapid annual increases in attendance. One of its secrets is to continually present something new, and to turn the Center into a local resource that a core of visitors keeps coming to over and over again, rather than just a repository that attendees see once or twice in their lifetime. The Center uses new exhibits, blockbuster lectures, partnerships with local institutions, privileges for members, aggressive capital expansion, e-marketing and an interactive website, among other strategies and tactics, to keep visitors coming back.

THE VERMONT HISTORICAL SOCIETY

BASIC DESCRIPTION OF THE VERMONT HISTORICAL SOCIETY

The Vermont Historical Society operates two facilities, a museum in Montpelier, and a headquarters facility based in a Richardsonian Romanesque historic schoolhouse constructed in 1890. The Society has a staff of 17 (FTE) and an annual budget of approximately $1.8 million. We spoke with Kevin Graffagnino, Director of the Vermont Historical Society. The Society receives state support but is considered a non-profit corporation.

Vermont is a history-conscious state, and its 251 towns and municipalities (230 with more than 50 people) maintain 190 local historical societies. "In Vermont everything is done on a town basis," says Graffagnino, "our biggest city is Burlington with 35,000 people. The town is the basic unit of municipal measure in Vermont; the State does not use the county as an organizing unit, common in most other states."

Graffagnino feels one of the Society's most important challenges is how to market without much of a marketing budget. The answer has been aggressive outreach to local schools, historical societies, local companies and other entities. Assertive cooperation has been the answer, a very Vermontonian answer at that.

As far as the official marketing budget, Graffagnino will only say "Occasionally we can afford to print a brochure."

STAFF IN MARKETING FUNCTIONS

Without much money for the hard sell, just about everyone become a salesman to some extent. The Society staff breaks down as follows:

"We have 2.5 positions in the library and 2.5 in the museum; three positions in membership and development and 2.5 positions in education and outreach. The education department has 2.5 positions and what we try to combine is working with Vermont schools and teachers. We provide Vermont history content. If a social-studies teacher wants to include Vermont material in a history module then they come to us."

A second target of the education/outreach is Vermont's many small local historical societies. Graffagnino feels that reaching out to them is critical to the organization's overall mission.

"Outreach is trying to provide the help and advice that small local historical societies need," he explains, "such as how to apply for grants and do preservation."

The Society further supports Vermont teachers by providing them with kits that illustrate and help teach Vermont history.

Graffagnino explains, "We have educational kits – big plastic jobs full of hands-on things such as replicas of artifacts, 18th- and 19th-century clothing items, replicas of original manuscripts or letters. The kits are big things; they are about three or four cubic feet. They are sent out for classroom use. It gives kids a sense of touching history, of handling it. They can say: 'My gosh, these are the utensils that 18th-century pioneers might have had to contend with.' "

The artifacts themselves tell a story and are organized according to different themes or periods in Vermont heritage: the Civil War, the Revolutionary War, the Underground Railroad, Vermont Industry, Vermont Agricultural History, Native-American History, Minorities Within the State, Ethnic Diversity Within the State, etc.

The Society runs a special state history day, and on that day hundreds of school kids descend on the City of Barry to view documents and exhibits.

"Kids can come to the state capital since Vermont is such a small state," says Graffagnino, "the first time they come will be in the fourth grade and then they come back in the seventh grade or 11th grade."

Vermont follows a highly decentralized approach to history instruction and does not mandate content as do many states. However, despite the absence of a state-mandated state history study, local Vermont teachers keep the Society quite occupied with information requests.

THE VERMONT HISTORICAL SOCIETY'S ROLE IN TOURISM

The Society closed its museum in Montpelier for two years while it moved its headquarters to Barry, but built a new exhibit in Montpelier that serves as a tourist draw. The Society tries to attract the tourist traffic coming to see the Montpelier statehouse. "In every state the statehouse is a local tourist draw," explains Graffagnino.

THE SOCIETY'S WEBSITE

"We have a fair-to-middling website that we are working to upgrade," says Graffagnino with a sigh. "I can't assign too many staff [to upgrade the site]. In Kentucky I had a staff of 90. Pennsylvania has 400, Minnesota has 90. But more and more people are visiting organizations like ours electronically. We have a committee together – including members of the board – and we are working on it, but our web manager is also our head librarian (and consequently has many other responsibilities). It is a question of time rather than ability."

DIGITIZATION

The Society has a vast collection of 100,000 historic photographs and 10,000 maps, broadsides, prints, and posters.

"We are digitizing it very slowly. We have very little of our own equipment. We have one research university in Vermont and we do some projects with them on a cooperative basis."

DRAMATICALLY SUCCESSFUL NEW FUNDRAISING EFFORT

The Society has recently raised an astounding $7.5 million, enabling it to construct new facilities and to develop new exhibits and major program enhancements. The Society was able to do this even though in the past it had never raised more than a few hundred thousand dollars.

"We tried to present a bold new vision and we have been successful in getting Vermonters to realize that it was not just the old organization." Graffagnino attributes the Society's great new success in fundraising to two relatively new projects that have dramatically raised the Society's statewide profile. The first is called the Community History Project.

THE COMMUNITY HISTORY PROJECT

How did the Vermont Historical Society make local history so avant-garde? "The state of Vermont reduced what it was doing in social studies," explained Graffagnino, and these educational cutbacks created a hole that would be filled by the Society. "We could say that we were the go-to organization for Vermont history. We started a project called the Community History Project. We became the brokers linking local historical societies to local schools."

It was a simple idea but one that provided the kindling for the many local history societies in Vermont. These societies, like their counterparts in many other states, have much to offer, but little in the way of funding or marketing know-how to reach out to local schools, veterans' organizations, businesses, and the general public. When the resources of local historical societies are presented to the public in an integrated and meaningful way the results can be astonishing. The project – in true Vermont fashion – was not really top-down, but kindled the firewood lying about in the local historical societies.

Graffagnino explains, "In Vermont you do not say that the central society orders the local organization to do anything. It is against the local tradition which is town-based. The project emphasized local history. What does it mean to be a resident? It brought the senior citizens, who predominate in the local history societies, and brought them together with their grandchildren. We became coordinators. I think it is a national model."

The Society seeks about 15 participants per year, and generally pairs local schools with their counterpart local historical societies. The local school-society partnerships submit project plans that in some way highlight local history.

"There is a two-year commitment from the local societies and schools," explains Graffagnino enthusiastically. "Some work in traditional ways. Some produce websites about local history. Others produce [museum-style] exhibits. One produced a play about local history. Plays, websites, and pamphlets, photo albums: we leave the product up to the local imagination and we try to guide a little. It all has a contagious energy. We bring all the districts together and kids in one town will see exhibits from other towns, they'll say, 'You should have seen what Burlington was doing!'"

The Vermont Historical Society gets support for the program from IBM and Verizon, which provide software, hardware, or funding. The annual cost of the entire program, encompassing all 15 projects, is about $150,000, which the Society supports entirely by private sector donations.

THE VERMONT HISTORY EXPO

A second major program that has raised the visibility of the Society, and helped it to raise money and better fulfill its mission is called the Vermont History Expo.

During the expo, the Society rents out a fairground, and invites local historical societies and museums to set up exhibits. One hundred and ten local historical societies and museums exhibited at the last Vermont History Expo; the event costs $7 for admission, and drew 8,000 visitors. More than 25% of the visitors are from out of the state, so the event is also a good tourist-oriented event for Vermont.

Typical exhibits include agriculture in town X, or sports in town Y, or the civil war in town Z. The expo has a budget of $155,000. The local societies are not charged for participation. There are exhibitors from every corner of the state

The exhibits are often graphic, fun, and interactive. An agricultural exhibit might feature merino sheep and draft horses, while another exhibit demonstrated 19th-century games.

"We played hoops," says Graffagnino, referring to a 19th-century skirt and dancing game," and I do not mean basketball. There are no video games but the kids have the time of their lives. After an hour or so the parents have to drag them away. Initially they are reluctant but then the kids get involved."

But it is not only the kids who are enthusiastic about the Vermont History Expo.

"The local societies that come get to check out the others. Each year the exhibits get better – the artifacts, photographs, quilts, civil war muskets."

The entire program is sponsored by local industry. One of the big sponsors is Vermont cheese-giant Cabot Cheese.

"A sponsor can give as little as $500. For insurance and real estate companies, 7,000 or 8000 people will learn about you if you sponsor this event."

ADVICE TO OTHER ORGANIZATIONS

Historical societies need to reach out, develop new and innovative approaches, and prove their relevance.

"The Community History Project and Vermont History Expo are very innovative program changes. And these events help us raise money since it has really increased our profile. So, people say, 'you are not just sleepy and dusty, you are a vibrant and alive organization.' Many adults are prone to say, 'I did not like history in school.' We like to say the Vermont Historical Society is about the past but our eyes are on the future. If you do not know the past, your solutions for tomorrow will not be as informed. One of my nephews called it history with muscle – which is a great phrase.

"I need an argument [to make with state authorities and donors]. Here, this is why we matter as much as marketing the ski industry, as much as the schools for our kids. I need an argument for people who are not history nuts."

HOOK'S HISTORICAL DRUG STORE AND PHARMACY

BASIC DESCRIPTION OF HOOK'S HISTORICAL DRUG STORE AND PHARMACY

Hook's Historical Drug Store and Pharmacy has been located as a permanent exhibit in the Indiana State Fair Ground since 1966. Originally, the exhibit was started as a private museum by the Hook Drug Company, which has since been purchased by major pharmacy retailers Revco and CVS. The museum is now self-supporting. We spoke with Julia Miller Moore, Director of Marketing and Communications for Hook's Historical Drug Store and Pharmacy.

The Drug Store Museum draws its visitors from the Indiana State Fair when it is in session; otherwise the organization's main revenue generator is a life science education program, mostly but not exclusively aimed at school children. The Museum has 2,500 square feet of exhibit space in which it has a complete recreation of a turn-of-the-century pharmacy, complete with patent medicines, various sodas (most of which were developed by pharmacists), weights and measures, pharmacists' tools, advertisements, and equipment and paraphernalia for different treatments. The Museum features original 1850s cabinetry and the famous glass paintings that once characterized the elegant American pharmacy.

The Organization's main focus is now the educational market, and it offers pre-packaged courses in the life sciences to grade-school and high-school students across the country. Hook's takes its hands-on programs directly into classrooms, mostly in middle schools, but in high schools a well. Hook's also offer pre-K and adult-education classes all focused in the life sciences. The website is: www@hooksdlc.org. Hooks has a staff of seven, most of whom are either accredited teachers or have some form of educational or science credentials, or both.

Hooks focuses on developing courses that help teachers to meet mandated, state-education coverage requirements, and provides the classes through interactive video conferencing, among other vehicles. Costs vary but average about $100.

The classes are very "hands-on" and look at how science relates to every day life. Some of the fields that Hooks has developed classes for are: Biology, Environmental Science, Forensics, Genetics, and Nuclear Pharmacy (radioactive pharmaceuticals). Hooks offers more than 30 educational programs. The programs are interactive and designed to catch attention. Beyond the educational market, Hooks also offers the programs to the Boy Scouts and Girl Scouts, offering courses that help members of these organizations to meet their badge requirements. In addition, Hooks does summer camps, after-school programs, and partners with Boys and Girls Clubs of America, and other organizations that reach out to school-age children and teens. One best selling program is: *THE BODY: gross, yucky and Oh SO Cool.* Participants receive instruction as well as interactive "course packs" that pull kids in and make learning interactive and engaging.

DISTANCE LEARNING

Ms Moore notes that the organization's distance learning efforts got its start through a grant from the Center for Interactive Learning and Collaboration (CILC – www.cilc.org), a non-profit organization in Indiana that assists schools, libraries and hospitals with videoconferencing technology and content.

SUMMER CAMP

In addition to its classes, Hook's started a summer science camp in 2002. Currently, it runs four one-week sessions, which have about 20 kids per session.

DIRECT MAIL & SPACE ADVERTISING

Moore says that Hook's mails a program guide once a year to middle and secondary school science teachers. It also has specialized programs, and partners in these ventures will market them with direct mail to their membership. For example, the organization has a program for senior citizens marketed by OAISIS, a senior-citizens' group. Hook's does not do much space advertising but does take out occasional ads in *Indy's Child*, a local Indiana children's magazine.

WEBSITE

Hook's has not done a great deal of web marketing but has redesigned its website. The informative site includes a science quiz and general information about the organization's programs.

MONTICELLO

BASIC DESCRIPTION OF THE THOMAS JEFFERSON FOUNDATION

Monticello is the original home of Thomas Jefferson; it is currently owned and operated by the Thomas Jefferson Foundation. The Foundation owns 2,300 acres of property surrounding Monticello, as well as the historic mansion itself. Jefferson owned 5,000 acres in this area. (Jefferson died broke and in debt and the property was sold off after his death) and the Foundation has managed to acquire close to half of Jefferson's original holdings.

The Foundation's mission is the preservation of both Monticello and the legacy of Thomas Jefferson, third president of the United States, diplomat, political thinker, author, horticulturalist, and architect. Monticello attracts 500,000 people per year. We spoke with Wayne Moglielnicki, Director of Communications for the Thomas Jefferson Foundation, which operates Monticello.

SCOPE OF THE THOMAS JEFFERSON FOUNDATION'S ACTIVITIES

The preservation and presentation of Jefferson's home is only one of the Foundation's missions. The Foundation has a highly active education department and also maintains the Robert H Smith International Center for Jefferson Studies.

"This is essentially our academic arm," explains Moglielnicki. "We have visiting fellows – both short term and long term – and we have a library and conferences. We also have a Center for Historic Plants – Jefferson was a big plant fan – he had a flower garden, an orchard, and he was very interested in horticulture. Many plants here at Monticello are heirloom and historical varieties."

The Foundation branches out in areas relevant to its mission and one of these is the fundamental archeology of the Monticello site.

"We have an archeology department that is investigating the grounds for artifacts. They have 'digs' and occasionally serve as consultants – the archeology staff numbers eight people full time," says Mogielnicki.

DIMENSIONS OF THE FOUNDATION

The Foundation's yearly operating budget is about $10 million, and the organization employs approximately 130 people full time year-round, and as many as 350 individuals during the peak summer season. This figure does not include visiting scholars or a handful of volunteers (currently, Monticello has just two volunteers). "Everyone is paid," says Mogielnicki.

IMPACT OF GEOGRAPHY ON MARKETING

Monticello is about 2½ hours from Washington and most visitors come for Monticello and do not combine the trip with side trips to other sites, at least not on the same day. "If we were located where Mt. Vernon is located then our marketing effort would be different," says Moglielnicki. Mt Vernon is located just outside of Washington DC. Monticello's somewhat more remote location makes joint marketing efforts with other local attractions a less enticing option than for many other major monuments and sites.

DECLINING ATTENDANCE

Monticello drew 458,865 people last year but the trend in attendance is down. "Attendance has dropped 13 of the past 15 years," says Moglielnicki. "We share this with numerous historic sites in this part of the country and elsewhere. Visitation has gone down for seven consecutive years – in 1997 it was 561,306."

Although attendance has fallen, and approximately 34% of revenue is derived from it, some of the shortfall in revenue has been made up by increasing admission prices and from rising sales of merchandise from retail sales, a gift shop, catalog, and online sales. Monticello derives about 36% of its revenue from product sales.

"We have raised admission prices but sales from the catalogs and gift shop have also gone up. In an effort to increase revenue the admission price went from $11 to $13, effective January 1 2003, and this year it went to $14 from $13. The children's rate has been the same for a number of years." Children under six enter free and local residents get a discount.

Monticello derives 14% of its revenue from gifts and grants and about 12% from interest income, through its endowment of about $60 million. Another 4% of total revenue comes from product licenses and other sources of income.

In addition to the operating income, the Foundation occasionally receives gifts and grants for capital or long-term projects. Recently the Robert H Smith International Center for Jefferson Studies received a $15 million gift, which will be awarded at the rate of $1 million per year for the next 15 years, substantially augmenting the endowment over time. The education department and the archeology department have also been recipients of major gifts or grants.

THE FOUNDATION'S PUBLISHING ARM

In addition to its substantial activities in education, scholarship, tourism, archeology and architecture, the Foundation maintains an active publishing arm in Jefferson-related publications.

Moglielnicki comments on a recent project, "A major project right now is the printed edition of Jefferson's papers in his retirement years, 1809 to 1826. The finished product will be published by Princeton University Press; it will be 23 volumes. The first one will be coming out in March 2005. Princeton University Press had started doing Jefferson's papers back in the 1940s – correspondence, notes, account books, etc. They published 30 volumes that go up to January 1799. So with an agreement with Princeton we took over the editing and compilation for the period from 1809 until his death. They hope to publish one volume per year."

More commonly, the Foundation publishes its own books, but they are distributed by the University of North Carolina Press. A typical recent book published by the Foundation was a coffee-table book on Monticello.

MARKETING

The Foundation has only a very small official advertising budget.

"We are not the most active marketing group. We have a very small advertising budget; for 2005 it is approximately $65,000. We rely very heavily on Jefferson's reputation and ours. We have been open since 1923, and we rely on the local convention visitor's bureau and the state [of Virginia]."

The Foundation is able to garner publicity through citations in articles in newspapers and magazines. The broad range of Jefferson's interests is the Foundation's best public relations weapon.

"Placement in newspapers and magazines, travel articles, and such – we generate those through hard work and good fortune. We do not have to build a reputation for the place or for Jefferson. We do not have to try to pitch or sell but we do try to be very responsive to the media – we will set things up within 24 hours, some historic sites well. You get it in six to eight weeks. If I were working at the home of Franklin Pierce I might have a different philosophy. But, because of Jefferson's interests, we get publicity in a wide variety of publications – travel, history, and government. We get the normal travel history stuff but Monticello is regarded as an architectural jewel. We get interest from architecture publications, and horticultural and agricultural [publications]. Jefferson was a pioneer in growing grapes and a big devotee of wine. We had *Cooking Light Magazine* here."

The broad range of Jefferson's interests and the impact he has had on a wide range of fields enables the Foundation to pursue public relations opportunities in a variety of publications, and careful targeting is the key to success.

"If we have something to publicize with our news releases we don't send something necessarily about an architectural restoration project to *Food and Wine*. For a garden symposium with a local speaker we do not send that to the *New York Times*. We try to tailor it to the right audience."

WEB MARKETING

Moglielnicki describes the Foundation's website (www.monticello.org) as "having two main purposes. One is for visitors, but it also is very popular with researchers, from kids to scholars working on some Jefferson research. It is a little different from websites at other historic places in that we keep the educational outreach in mind."

The emphasis on educational outreach keeps Monticello and Jefferson in the minds of researchers and enhances the Jefferson image, and the fortunes of Monticello.

TRADITIONAL ADVERTISING VEHICLES

Monticello uses very little traditional advertising, such as space ads, radio, and television. It has used local radio for holiday evening tours, which are considered special local events since Monticello generally closed at 5 P.M., even on weekends. Virtually all traditional space-ad and radio advertising is for locally oriented events. The Foundation does some advertising in travel directories and magazines, and does cooperative ads with the local convention and visitors' bureau.

The organization does not have cooperative deals with airlines or hotels. "We are really a half-day attraction," says Moglielnicki, and visitors tend to stay about two to three hours. There is not much else around here – except the University of Virginia and most of the attractions around here are kind of low key. It is a wonderful place to visit but it is not Orlando or Las Vegas. If we were located where Mt. Vernon is we might have a different philosophy. We have guided tours but we have no costume guides or characters on the grounds; no one is dressed up as Thomas Jefferson."

REVAMPED CATALOG

The Foundation recently revamped its catalog, reducing the print run and limiting the number of products offered through the catalog.

"At one point it [the catalog] sort of got too big. They were sending out untold millions of them four times per year. The catalog included stuff that had no direct tie to Monticello or Jefferson. A few years ago, in 2002, we scaled back the catalog operation. We were sending it out four times per year, a [cumulative four-year] total of six million [direct mail pieces]. Now just once a year, two different editions are sent out to a [cumulative] total of one million. We also cut back on the range of products in the catalog and restricted it to products connected to Monticello or Jefferson. The profit margin on the expanded mailing was very, very small and by scaling it back we are making the same amount of money or more but spending a lot less – plus philosophically getting back to our core attachments. We still have garden products, for example, but they are more related to the science of those times – the design of the flowerpot is from Jefferson's era, something that you would find at Monticello."

MARKETING TO SCHOOLS

As might be expected, Monticello is a big lure for school groups. The Foundation's education department sends out a schedule of education tours to local schools as well as schools throughout the United States, focusing especially on those that have visited Monticello previously. The schedule of tours is also a poster for which the Foundation commissions an original watercolor. Often, the tours sell out and the schools that visit often sign up on the spot to return the next year. In early February when this interview was conducted, Monticello had "sold out" its space for school tours.

Although the Foundation does direct mail to schools, it relies heavily on word of mouth and repeat business. The education department does attend some education-related trade shows, such as that of the American Association of Teachers of History.

School tours are highly seasonal in nature. "Schools do not go anywhere in September or in May," says Moglielnicki, "and October, November, February, March, and April are the peak season. School tours and summer tourists compose the two largest cohorts of visitors. We get 75% of our visitors in April, May, June, July, August, and October – in six months. March and September would be the next two [months ranked by attendance]. In January, we had 800 the entire month but in summer we can get 2,500 or more on a single day. We would like to try to spread it out."

MARKETING IN EUROPE

Since Jefferson served as US Minister to France from 1784 to 1789 and was known as a Francophile, we asked if there were any special marketing efforts to attract French visitors.

"We are more popular with visitors from England, Germany, and Japan than France," says Moglielnicki. "Jefferson was a Francophile and lived there but we have had only a few French journalists here. We have had far more from Germany, Japan, England, and Italy."

Despite Jefferson's international fame, no foreign country accounts for more than 1.2% of Monticello's visitors. In the most recent year, visitors from foreign countries accounted for about 5% of total visitors, including visitors from Canada.

PATRIMONY ISSUE

Since Jefferson's legacy was recently shaken by the genetic evidence pointing to the truth of his love affair with his slave Sally Hemmings, we asked Moglielnicki about the impact that the well publicized findings had on Monticello and the Foundation's overall mission.

"The Sally Hemmings issue does not really affect attendance," he explains. "When it originally happened we lost some donors. On the other hand we probably gained just as many who appreciated the fact that we would admit such a thing. We got a lot of news coverage – some viewed it as a positive and some viewed it as a negative, and some don't care. That is one of the other issues in addition to architecture, astronomy, etc, that have kept Jefferson in the spotlight. For a while that was the most frequently sought-after topic [by inquirers from the media] by a wide margin."

ADVICE FOR OTHER ORGANIZATIONS

"We have fond that each site is unique and each one has very different facilities, capabilities, goals, and resources. We share information and we are members of the Virginia Association of Museums, and the American Association of Museums. In terms of advice for some formula to get more visitors – any blanket statement would be trite. We try to always keep true to our mission, our purpose, our standards. We are not going to boost attendance by having a laser lightshow or a rock concert. We do not ever allow Monticello to be rented out for parties or weddings and we do not allow it to be used as a backdrop for fashion shoots."

THE MUSEE CONTI

BASIC DESCRIPTION OF THE MUSEE CONTI

It is easy to poke fun at the kitsch of wax museums but they are one of the great original ways to market basic history to the broader population of Americans, and remain popular attractions that can graphically impart historical knowledge to those who might not seek it out in other venues.

The Musee Conti Wax Museum, founded in 1964, recounts the history of New Orleans through wax figures of some of its most famous residents, including Louis Armstrong, Andrew Jackson, Huey Long, and Marie Laveau, a notorious voodoo priestess. It spans 300 years of New Orleans history through 154 wax figures with accompanying décor and audio and visual explanations of history. In order to draw more children, the Museum added a haunted dungeon with mythical characters such as Frankenstein and Dracula, among others. We spoke with Beth Sigur, Sales Manager for the Musee Conti.

The cost for admission to the Wax Museum and haunted dungeon is $6.75 for adults and $5.75 for children. The 8,000 square foot facility, located in New Orleans' famed French Quarter draws tourists and school groups. Its historic motifs and French Quarter location make it a favored place for meetings and banquets for major companies and other organizations.

ORIGINS OF THE WAX MUSEUM

All of the Museum's wax figures were made in France; the glass eyes are made in Germany and the (truly human) hair is imported from Italy. Pierre Imans, a major figure in the wax-museum world, came over from France to New Orleans to personally arrange the presentation of the wax figures in the 1960s. Just a few new figures have been added over the past 40 years to keep up with New Orleans' developing history. Some new characters are former governor Edwin Edwards, and musician Pete Fountain.

ATTENDANCE

As with many historically oriented attractions, the Musee Conti caters to students as well as tourists. The Louisiana school curriculum includes requirements for the study of Louisiana state history in the eighth grade, and the Museum gets many organized visits from eighth-graders studying state history. Typical visitors spend about 1½ hours in the museum and visits are actually built into the curriculum of some Louisiana school districts.

MARKETING EFFORTS

Marketing efforts focus on close relations with the local convention and visitors' bureau and attendance at travel-oriented trade shows. Musee Conti sends emissaries to trade shows sponsored by the National Tour Association, the American Bus Association, Travel South, Meeting Planners International, and Incentive Travel and Meeting Executives. The organization also sends brochures to Louisiana teachers and sends coupons to local hotels and concierge desks, including specialized coupons for some local hotels. The Museum is also a member of the Louisiana Travel Promotion Association.

On the whole, Ms. Sigur feels that attendance at conventions is the best way to sell the Museum, even though she often encounters a bit of condescension to wax museums.

"We sometimes have a booth but sometimes it is hard to sell a wax museum, a lot of times people have a negative opinion. But the shows are huge. That is where you get all of your tour and travel and incentive houses – all of your big incentive companies."

The Museum has done well by marketing itself to incentive travel companies that offer packaged trips to companies as rewards for good employee performance. Such companies are often looking for good package deals on transportation, accommodations and entertainment. They can steer travel to particular sites and attractions by including them in packages or simply listing them in travel promotions or itineraries.

Special events are a big revenue earner for the Museum.

"We have done as few as one event a month and as many as 17. It is such a huge way of increasing your revenue and we have the space since we have the upstairs too. We are located in the French Quarter."

THE MUSEUM'S WEBSITE

The Museum puts its floor plan on the website, "as well as pictures of all of our events, and all of the options for décor. We have a bunch of different décor options such as the 'Spirit of New Orleans'. The Museum did the website with its own personnel, and the Museum does some forms of web marketing. Email follow-ups from trade show contacts have been effective. The website is at www.get-waxed.com.

THE BOSTONIAN SOCIETY

BASIC DESCRIPTION OF THE BOSTONIAN SOCIETY

The Bostonian Society is a historic site, museum and archive devoted to local City of Boston history. The Society has an annual operating budget of $1.5 million, and a full-time staff of seven. The entrance fee is $5 for adults and $1 for Massachusetts school children, seniors and tour guides, and children under six years of age.

The Society was founded in 1881 by a group of Bostonians to save the old state house. We spoke with Susan Goganian, Site Director for the Bostonian Society.

MARKETING

The Society makes only modest marketing efforts, and benefits greatly from tapping into the enormous tourist flow into Boston. Its public relations efforts include calendar listings and press releases to the *Boston Globe*, a few neighborhood weeklies, and a group of newspapers called the TAB that have versions in local neighboring towns.

"The listings in the *Globe* help significantly," says Goganian, "and sometimes the others help a lot. We are also listed on [the newspaper's] internet sites."

The Society has had its own website for five years and in this period has hired graphic designers twice for alterations. The site URL is www.bostonhistory.org.

EXHIBITS

In addition to the old state house itself, the Society has a formidable collection of Boston memorabilia. One recent exhibit – *Every Picture Tells a Story* – featured photographs from the Society's extensive collection of 35,000 Boston-related photographs. Most of the photographs in the exhibit featured Boston neighborhoods over the past 100 years.

In addition to local listings, the Society advertises its exhibitions on its website and through its print and online newsletters. The Society mails out its newsletter to about 1,500 subscribers each year, including local libraries, museums and universities – which themselves may publicize the Society's events.

MERCHANDISE SALES

The Society has annual merchandise sales exceeding $800,000, mostly of merchandise related to Boston. Popular items include books, toys, images, plates, mugs, aprons, ornaments, teapots and teacups, and other ceramic objects.

Books are big sellers and the Society offers between 200 and 300 titles for sale. Books on sports history, particularly the Boston Red Sox, are the best sellers. Books on the revolutionary war period and the run up to it in Boston are also good sellers. Children's books on the revolution are good sellers. However, enthusiasm for other sports or for independence from the British Empire does not exceed Red Sox fever.

"We have a lot of books about the Red Sox," says Goganian, "We don't have anywhere near as many books about the Celtics, and I don't think I have ever seen a book about the Bruins (the Boston professional hockey team), we have a few books on the Patriots but mostly it is the Red Sox."

VISITORS

About 35% of the Society's visitors are from outside the country and maybe 45% are from states other than Massachusetts. Only 20% are from Massachusetts and less than half of those are from Boston.

The Society relies on the local visitors' and convention bureau, the Boston National Historical Park (part of the Federal Park's Service) and other such organizations for referrals. It develops brochures related to particular programming and largely markets through its own newsletter, listings and distribution of the brochures through related organizations.

RENTAL OF FACILITIES

Facilities rental is, in the words of Goganian, "part of what we do to support our mission. It is not huge for us. We have some weddings here, we have meetings; we have corporate dinners. We have a variety of office functions, office parties, and anyone who has an event here can look around the museum."

DIGITIZATION OF THE SOCIETY'S ASSETS

The Society is in the process of digitizing its extensive photography collection.

"We are doing it in house," explains Goganian, "We got funding to start the project. We have a high quality scanner and the software we are using is called Rediscovery. It is really worth it – it is making out collection accessible to anyone – it is on our website. It increases the number of people who have access to our library."

ADVICE FOR SIMILAR ORGANIZATIONS

"I would say that the more you can get yourself out there [the better] – which you can do by collaborating with other institutions, or by doing something new. It is difficult for a small organization without someone dedicated to marketing to be successful. "

THE DITTRICK MEDICAL HISTORY CENTER

BASIC DESCRIPTION OF THE DITTRICK MEDICAL HISTORY CENTER

The Dittrick Medical History Center, housed at Case Western Reserve University, in Cleveland, Ohio, is one of the oldest medical history museums in the United States. We spoke with James Edmonson, Chief Curator of the Dittrick Medical History Center.

In 1898, the Cleveland Medical Library Association, recently incorporated in 1894, decided to form a historical committee to make plans for the member library's holdings of rare books and other medical items of historic interest and other items. When the Association decided to build a new headquarters, they included in the design a third floor gallery to showcase the Association's holdings that were of historic interest.

"This was a reflection of the interests of Dr. Dudley Peter Allen, a prominent member of the Board of the Library and a distinguished surgeon in Cleveland and he developed an avocational interest in the history of medicine," explains Mr. Edmonson. "He married Elizabeth Severance and her father Louis Severance was the main business partner of John D Rockefeller. He became a collector of medical things that documented the history of medicine in the 1790s through to the 1850s. He gave them to the Library and a local surgeon named Gustaf Webber later also gave two large collections of surgical instruments. The material started to accumulate and, upon the death of Dr. Allen in 1915, his widow made a bequest to the Library Association and proposed to fund a new building. The third floor contains a museum gallery at the stipulation of Mrs. Allen. I can only think of one other association that had a medical museum at the time – the College of Physicians in Philadelphia – when the building was opened in 1926. The responsibility for the collection fell to Howard Dittrick who also had an avocational interest in the history of medicine. He was an avid collector and in those days medical antiques did not have a big monetary value, so people gave the instruments that had been in their family. His phase [of museum stewardship] was focused on collecting and he derived inspiration from Henry Wellcome. Wellcome had a successful business career in Great Britain and he collected thousands of objects related to the history of medicine and today that material is featured in the science museum in London."

In 1997 control of the museum was transferred from the Case Western University medical library over to the college of arts and sciences of Case Western University.

NEW COLLECTION RELATED TO CONTRACEPTIVE HISTORY

The Museum has just been the recipient of a major gift: the Percey Skuy Collection on the History of Contraception which is "the world's largest collection of historic materials on contraception," says Edmonson. The gift promises to dramatically raise the museum's profile. Indeed, in the six months prior to the acquisition of this collection, the museum's website received 25,000 hits, while in the single month after it announced the acquisition, it received 45,000 hits.

THE ACQUISITION OF THE PERCEY SKUY COLLECTION

Percy Skuy was the CEO of Ortho Pharmaceutical in Toronto. The company manufactured IUD's and other contraceptive products and when Skuy retired about five years ago, he decided that the collection, which was housed at the Janssen Ortho production facility, should go to a museum or educational institution. Dittrick management saw it as an opportunity to expand its collection.

"We put together a prospectus outlining what we would do with it," explained Edmonson. "Basically it outlines that we would acquire and display the collection and work with faculty and that we would develop courses that use and feature research projects by students and faculty using the collections."

About a half-dozen faculty members met with Percy. Edmonson smiles, "He was here trying to sell us on why we should get it and we were trying to sell him on why he should give it to us."

Skuy donated the collection, which was fortunate for the Museum since the cost of medical antiques has risen sharply in recent years.

"He worked with an appraiser in Toronto to come up with a value and use that as a basis for a charitable donation," said Edmonson, who emphasized Skuy's determination to see the collection used in an educational context. Edmonson notes that it has become more difficult to build medical history collections, as the plethora of medical museums worldwide, and the emergence of serious and well funded collectors of medical devices and paraphernalia of medical interest, has buoyed prices and made it difficult for medical museums without large endowments or great resources.

"We do not have the money to become players in that area," says Edmonson, referring to the commercial markets for antique medical devices. "Now there are at least a half-dozen websites for medical antiques. The premium dollar goes for civil war–era medical antiques. The highest price I saw for a civil-war era surgical set was $27,000 for one with good provenance, which is everything of value for medical instruments."

MARKETING OF THE MUSEUM

The Museum, which is open 10 A.M. to 5 P.M. Monday to Friday, gets about 25,000 visitors annually, many of them local. Marketing efforts have tended to focus on the local area's medical community, particularly those in medical research. The Cleveland area has several major medical research institutions, and so do nearby major cities such as Columbus and Cincinnati.

The Museum works with the University's marketing staff, and with the public relations and marketing consulting firms hired by the University.

"There is someone at the Case campus PR office who works for the College of Arts and Sciences, and the museum is on her beat, and she interacts with the national PR firm (Weber Shandwick based in Minneapolis), and also with different agencies. When she thinks that they might have an interest, she will contact them. She secured the contacts with the *Los Angeles Times* and they had their Midwest reporter based in St Louis, and they spent the better part of the day here talking to us. Subsequently we had similar things – the *Cleveland Plain Dealer* did a story when the collection came here, and that was picked up by other newspapers that they were affiliated with."

WEBSITE

The Museum's website, first implemented in 1994, underwent a major change in the past year. The University has worked with PR firm Yamamoto Moss on the branding of the University and Yamamoto encouraged a re-branding of all the University websites. The University changed its logo and mandated certain style sheets in the look of websites; part of this was done to keep in conformity with standards to help the visually impaired. "They introduced cascading style sheets – a form of web design," explained Edmonson. "It did affect out overall look – the format has a kind of corporate look about it. I think that this uniformity is happening all over the place. Our website looks more like a CNN website."

Over the past ten years, the Museum has not put too much of the collection on the website. However, this may change.

"For the museum itself we have a sampler collection. We have six to eight objects and tell the story behind them. We do not feel that having all the artifacts online is necessary. We have over 50,000 objects and how many viewers, quite honestly, will want to see 20,000 surgical instruments? We try to give a flavor of the place."

The Museum plans a more aggressive web strategy for the new contraceptive collection.

"With the contraceptive collection we may put up a complete catalog because it is a unique collection and probably the most comprehensive in the world," explains Edmonson. He also wants to add significantly to the explanatory materials that now accompany the older exhibits and the new contraceptive collection.

The Museum has also started to archive its exhibits online, providing a historic record of the types of special exhibits it has had in the past. The addition of the contraceptive collection has given the Museum the impetus to increase its national marketing, albeit in imaginative but inexpensive ways. As with many small museums, cooperation and cross marketing is the key.

"With this contraceptive collection we are moving in the direction of national marketing. We have initiated contacts with the American College of Obstetrics and Gynecology and we have been in correspondence with the World Congress of Obstetrics and Gynecology in Australia and the Royal College of Obstetrics and Gynecology. I have visited to the Museum of Contraception in Vienna."

Edmonson expects that the collection will be popular among other museums as well and he has already been approached by one.

"We have a regular policy of loaning objects to other museums for exhibitions. There is a Museum of Sex in New York City and they are looking for an oral contraceptive dispenser, a circular thing that keeps track of the daily dosage of the oral contraception."

Normally, the Museum does not have much money for marketing, but along with the contraceptive collection came a monetary gift that will be partially used for promotion.

Edmonson expects also that the University will want to see the new, special collection promoted but emphasizes that, as part of a larger institution, the Museum takes some its lead from University administration.

"We work through the University; we are part of a larger institution and things have to be vetted by the PR office. They want to make sure we are putting our best foot forward and putting the institution in the best possible light. The new collection has a fairly high profile."

EMAIL MARKETING

The Museum does not do extensive email marketing but does produce a newsletter in paper form that it sends to members of the Cleveland Medical Library Association, as well as to Friends of the Dittrick Museum, and to the members of the Medical Museum Association. The Museum hopes to create an online version of this newsletter.

THE MEDICAL MUSEUM ASSOCIATION & OTHER PARTNERS

The American Association for the History of Medicine and the American Medical Museum Association have been useful marketing partners. Many historically oriented museums can benefit from cross marketing simply because the common visitor to the Civil War Museum of North Carolina is a good prospect for the Civil War Museum of South Carolina as well.

In 1984 Edmonson attended a meeting of the European Association of Medical History Museums; US medical museums based at Harvard, the Smithsonian, and the College of Surgeons in Philadelphia, and Dittrick typically went to such meetings. The meeting became the genesis of the American Medical Museum Association.

"We developed a list of medical museums in the USA and Canada and in 1986 the Association was formed. We now have 60 or 70 members and it piggy-backs on the annual meeting of the American Association for the History of Medicine, itself an organization of historians, physicians, and archivists which draws 450 to 500 people [to its annual meeting]."

For about 10 years the American Medical Museum Association published a journal *CADUCEUS.*

"It was published out of the medical humanities department at Southern Illinois University; that source of support dried up and the journal proved not to be self sustaining."

LONDON AS MEDICAL MUSEUM MECCA

In addition to spreading the word about the Dittrick Museum to other medical museums and medical history societies around the globe, Edmonson has returned the favor by organizing tours of other museums for friends and patrons of the Dittrick Museum, or indeed anyone with an interest in medical history. London, England, has been a popular destination.

"In London there is an organization of medical and health museums and there are 20 collections or museums that you can visit in that one city." Edmonson worked with the author of *Weir's Guide to Medical Museums in the UK* to put together a tour for medical school alumni and associated fellow travelers. "Our Museum collaborated with Collander Travel and the Case Western Alumni Graduates, and it was mostly marketed to physicians and their spouses. Collander Travel put in ads through Ohio Triple A, and I posted announcements on a couple of different medical history listservs, one was Caduseus, a listserv out of Johns Hopkins, and another was for librarians and archivists, sponsored by the Association of Archivists and Librarians, on the history of the health sciences."

ORIGINS OF VISITORS TO THE MUSEUM

About three-quarters of visitors come from the general Cleveland area, particularly from two major research hospitals, the Cleveland Clinic and General University Hospital. The Museum makes particularly strenuous efforts to attract young interns from these institutions.

BUDGET & EMPLOYEES

The University pays the salaries and fringe benefits of three full-time employees, the director/curator, a registrar/archivist, and a web designer/photographer. Beyond this, the University provides about $22,000 annually for incidental expenses such as buying new boxes for archival materials or publishing invitations for the two lectures.

LECTURES & SPECIAL EVENTS

The Museum holds two special lectures per year. One is the Zverina lecture and "that lecture enables us to bring to campus a historian or museum curator that is doing history on medical technology. We have had many distinguished historians of medicine," explains Edmonson. The Museum started a second lecture series in 2000 called the Handerson Medical History Lectures.

"We used to have a group about called the Handerson Medical History Society but over time that group tended to thin out by attrition. There were many older people that had an avocational interest in the history of medicine but the younger generation of people are less interested in hearing historical lectures. Our lectures typically attract 50 to 60 people. We have a lecture coming up on March 31 and we are having the director of the medical history museum in Copenhagen give a talk about the development of their museum."

Edmonson schedules many of the lectures involving overseas participants or lecturers in early spring, to take advantage of the low airfares common at that time of year. The overall cost of bringing in a paid speaker from Europe can be as low as $1,500.

"In March the airfares are so low that we can bring them here for less than it costs to bring someone in from Minneapolis, and we can interact in a meaningful way," explains Edmonson. "It costs $400 to $450 for a round trip, and we give them a small honorarium – maybe $500. I have them arrive here on Wednesday evening and depart some time on Sunday. Usually, they give their talk on Thursday evening, and on Friday I take them to see other museums in Cleveland such as our Natural History Museum with its fine anatomical collection. On Saturday we may go out to Amish country or they might go to the Rock and Roll Hall of Fame or the Cleveland Museum of Art."

Four nights in a local hotel generally costs from $90 to $130 per night, and the Museum benefits from a university discount with the local hotels.

ADVICE

Edmonson emphasizes the role that a university-sponsored museum should play in support of the educational mission.

"You have to be seen as an asset to the larger institution, you have to be entrepreneurial and sell them on the idea that they should use the collection in their courses. It is best to target the young professors that have recently come to campus. If someone has been at the university for 10 to 15 years they are not about to re-tailor their courses to use the collection, but new faculty are more open.

Let me give you two examples. We have an instructor named Patricia Princehouse who teaches evolutionary biology – *Darwin's View of Life* [the name of the course]. In this course, the students will read a biography of Darwin and we have 179 letters of Charles Darwin's correspondence and students can do a research project based on these original 19th-century manuscripts. It is pretty cool to work with primary materials from a scientist of this caliber. Another instructor, Rene Sentilles, teaches in the history department and she teaches a class on women in medicine with a focus on the 19th century. She has students select from our collection an object relating to women's health.

It is a challenge to work with objects directly for the students – in both of these instances these are people at the beginning of their academic career, and they are interested in using objects that animate their instruction."

THE BAND MUSEUM

GENERAL DESCRIPTION OF THE BAND MUSEUM

The Band Museum was founded in 1994 by Jerry Horne, a Pine Bluff, Arkansas, resident and music enthusiast, now Director and Curator of the Band Museum. The Band Museum is an excellent example of how a small city can develop a regional tourist attraction by tapping into its reservoir of local history.

The City of Pine Bluff (population circa 100,000) donated a vintage 1890 three-story building, and Mr. Horne donated his extensive personal collection of vintage wind and percussion instruments, and the Band Museum was born. The Museum focuses on the types of instruments generally found in a high-school or college band.

The Museum particularly features the development of wind instruments and many of the exhibits show wind instruments at different stages in their development. "I have flutes in every stage of their development since 1715," says Horne.

Horne started with a personal collection of 500 instruments and now has about 1,500, some of which he purchased, while others were donated. "I got a lot of the instruments form the 1940s and 1950s donated," says Horne, "but it is the older ones and the oddball ones that are more desirable as tourist attractions. The public likes the screwball stuff like a signal horn with sixteen balls or a flute with only one key, and they also like the older instruments. I have an original saxophone by Adoloph Sachs, who invented the saxophone."

The Museum features instruments from mid-20th-century celebrities such as the cornet of Mearl Evans, the director of the Barnum & Bailey circus band, and instruments that once belonging to Charlie Spivak – a big band leader from the 30s and 40s. "We have saxophones from Louis Jordan, who played mostly in the 1940s. He was really the first rock and roller. He did rock and roll but they called it rhythm and blues because he was black," explains Horne. "The type of music he played was really rock and roll and a little blues. He played things like *Caledonia* and *Is You Is My Baby?* – stuff like that."

In addition to the instruments, Horne has local memorabilia from local bands such as those from Pine Bluff High School, Whitehall High School and Central High School from Little Rock. The Museum boasts about 500 artifacts such as plaques and loving cups as well as 300 to 350 photographs of old bands from the region. The artifacts are mostly restricted to Arkansas-interest while the instruments are from all over the country and abroad.

The Museum uses the first floor of the 18,000-square-foot building for exhibitions. The second floor has a rehearsal space with a stage and a meeting room with a sound system. It is often rented out for big band dances and rehearsals. The third floor is used mostly for storage since Horne can display at any one time only about 300 of the Museum's total inventory of 1,500 instruments. Horne rotates the displays so "if you come twice a year you will still see something different from the last time," he says.

The Museum is open from 10 A.M. to 4 P.M. Monday through Friday – or on weekends by special arrangement or tours – and attracts about 8,000 to 9,000 visitors annually.

ORIGINAL 1940s DRUG STORE

Mr. Horne came up with a novel idea for food service in the Museum. "This building housed the first soda fountain in this county. That soda fountain is still fully functional – it also housed the first electric elevator in this county, and it still operates."

The soda fountain serves milk shakes, ice-cream sodas, banana splits, and sundaes made in the original drug-store, soda-fountain style, including the original ingredients.

"I do a malted milk from scratch," says Horne, "you have a metal can and put in milk and flavors and ice cream on top of that, and you put it in an old Hamilton Beach mixer. Most people nowadays think their milkshakes are just soft ice cream – mine are mixed with real flavors and real ice cream. The flavors are chocolate or vanilla, or pure banana or cherry – and we make ice cream sundaes – it is just like it was back in the 1940s and 1950s. You have to be at least 50 to know what a soda fountain is. When I grew up there was a soda fountain in every drug store in every town."

In addition to drawing visitors, the old soda fountain still manages to satisfy the sweet tooth of local residents for special catering projects. For example, the local symphony orchestra has their desserts catered by the Band Museum's soda fountain shop.

"But most of the rest of our customers are grandmothers and grandfathers," says Horne, "and they bring their grandchildren in to let them see what a real soda fountain is."

MARKETING EFFORTS

As a very small museum that does not even charge admission, the Band Museum does not have much of a marketing budget, but it does benefit from listings in Arkansas state travel brochures and AAA listings. Arkansas has 14 state tourism centers and the Museum has brochures on file with all of them. When asked how the small museum got into the AAA guide, Horne explains, "They approached me, actually. I don't really remember how. Some guy just came to town and saw us and saw I had many people come by."

The Band Museum is also listed in a regional Southwest travel guide published in Oklahoma. The local convention center also included the Museum in its brochure that it distributes to thousands of inquirers and potential visitors to the region.

The Museum has attracted some foreign visitors and one useful tactic has been to advertise to student foreign-exchange associations, since such students often want to view the local sites of cultural interest.

Horne is also a member of the American Musical Instruments Society, a group of scholars and collectors that study antique and vintage musical instruments.

In the end, word-of-mouth and the Museum's more than 1,500 instruments are its best marketing tools. And one key audience tends to find it without encouragement.

"It attracts more musicians than anything else," says Horne. "They see that I have 1,500 instruments. But in the end this is just a two-person operation and we are limited in what we can do."

The website is at www.bandmuseum.org.

THE BELMONT MANSION

HISTORIC BACKGROUND OF THE BELMONT MANSION

Belmont Mansion was built in 1853 as the summer home of Joseph and Adelicia Acklen, prominent local citizens. She was the daughter of Oliver Bliss Hayes, an early settler of Nashville. Joseph was from Huntsville, Alabama and the grandson of John Hunt who founded the City of Huntsville. We spoke with Mr. Mark Brown, Executive Director of the Belmont Mansion

The house was enlarged in 1856 and enlarged and remodeled again in 1859 and 1860; the architect of the remodeling was Adopohus Heiman. In 1887 Belmont was sold to a land development company, which later sold the house and 13 acres to two ladies from Philadelphia who began a women's school in the fall of 1890. The women's school continued until 1951 and was first called the Belmont College for Young Women. In 1913 it merged with Ward Seminary, which had operated in Nashville since 1865, and the merged unit became known as Ward-Belmont. Ward-Belmont was sold to the current institution in 1951, and the merged co-ed entity became known as Belmont University, which now boasts nearly 4,000 graduate and undergraduate students. The University is affiliated with the Tennessee Baptist Convention and is particularly noted for its music and business programs.

The Belmont Mansion is built in the distinctive Italian Style – an extremely rare style in the United States. The size of the historic house eventually reached 36 rooms in over 21,000 square feet. At one time it was a 180-acre pleasure estate, though currently it is situated on the campus of Belmont University, in Nashville, TN. The building is owned by the University but operated by a private organization, the Belmont Mansion Association, formed in 1972. The property was opened to the public in 1976. The original grounds surrounding the Mansion are now part of the University campus but they still contain all five of the cast-iron gazebos as well as the original marble fountain, and some of the original cast-iron statuary.

The site attracts about 20,000 visitors annually; the admission charge is $8 per person.

ANNUAL BUDGET

The Organization's annual budget is $250,000 and it has two full-time and 18 part-time staff. Mostly the part-time staff are tour guides, housekeepers, and seasonal or special event employees.

MARKETING

The Belmont Mansion takes advantage as much as possible of all the free listings in the travel industry such as those offered through the Convention and Visitors' Bureau, and Tennessee State guides, as well as the AAA.

The Mansion also does a small amount of paid advertising and card-pack advertising to appeal for local motor-coach traffic and travel through the Convention & Visitors' Bureau. It had done a small amount of radio advertising in local markets adjoining Nashville, mostly within a day's drive of the Belmont Mansion. However, when management could not see any trackable results from the paid and quid-pro-quo radio advertising, it was discontinued. The Mansion also advertises through local area discount entertainment books.

SPECIAL EVENTS MARKETING

As might be expected, the Belmont Mansion is an especially appealing venue for weddings and other special events. The Mansion hosts about 30 weddings per year, and to advertise its availability as a wedding site Belmont advertises in local wedding-planner guides. The University uses the Mansion for special events such as concerts, poetry readings, opera and some lectures. The Nashville Battlefield Preservation Society meets in the Mansion six times per year, as do some other local community groups.

Belmont University is an alcohol-free campus and the restrictions on selling alcohol do pose some barriers in marketing the Mansion as a venue for corporate events. "However, we get some religious record companies renting it either for post-concert receptions or record-release parties since there is a large Christian music community in the USA so we get some groups like that renting it," says Brown.

MARKETING TO BANK TRAVEL GROUPS

Brown believes that marketing to bank travel groups has been an important strategy for the Belmont Mansion. He explains: "A lot of banks, particularly in smaller towns, offer a travel program to a certain level of depositor, and that is a real growing segment of the travel business. These depositors will pay to go on these trips and they have bank officials traveling with them – so that is a real big, growing market. Well the banks have an association for bank travel – the National Association of Bank Travel, something like that. We have bought advertising in their publications. Church groups are a good travel segment as well and we have done some direct-mail marketing to church groups with limited success."

CHRISTMAS SEASON TRAVEL

Belmont does not extensively tap into the national tourism market except that, as Brown notes, "We do well with the holiday-season traveler, Christmas season. We do very well with that group and we often have companies that do repeat business with us for the Christmas season, but not otherwise. A lot of the motor-coach traffic is geared towards country music, with the exception of the Christmas traffic."

DIRECT MAIL, PRESS & PUBLICITY

The Belmont Mansion takes advantage of a free, electronic press-release service offered by the Tennessee Department of Tourism. Brown is enthusiastic about the program.

"They will distribute it for you to target markets. They will even write it for you, if you want them to. We usually send out probably about three to four per year, depending on what is happening. We do direct mail to all of the leads provided by the Nashville Convention and Visitors Bureau."

WEBSITE

The Belmont Mansion initially put up its website about nine years ago; the first website was done through the University. After a few years, the Mansion decided to use a website offered by Citysearch.

Brown explains the rationale, "It is a national company that sets up in certain cities and they set up a city search that offers all different types of info, especially travel and entertainment–type activities. We did that for three years. They found us. When they came into Nashville they did aggressive marketing to the tourist attractions in the area; it worked out very well. We had a good number of hits but we then needed to develop it to do more than just the tourist traffic. We needed to make changes more often and we needed to add rental info. One of our staff members' husbands is a web designer and then we hired him."

Belmont spent $500 upgrading the site and added interactive features that enabled individuals to become members of the Foundation online. Brown says that the next step is to add an online gift shop, noting that the software that enabled them to implement the online-membership option will also enable them to develop the online gift shop.

Brown feels that it is especially important for Belmont to have an interactive online presence since many members of the Foundation are alumni of Belmont University or the old Ward-Belmont, and do not necessarily live in the Nashville area. These people can keep in touch through cyberspace. "It's a little unusual for a site such as ours to have its membership (currently about 700) scattered all over the USA," says Brown.

According to Brown, the more extensive website has helped in numerous other ways. "It is pretty amazing. Anytime we do membership solicitations we are now referring them to our website. People find those websites – people are increasingly finding us online."

ADVICE FOR OTHER HISTORIC SITES

"We have found that the public programming has great benefits in increasing the walk-in visitation traffic. If you have a limited advertising budget and if you are trying to get the local market, a public-programming opportunity translates into visitation increases all the time and not just for the event. We recently had out 150th anniversary and we tried to do one event per month and we had the best attendance year ever. I stay away from lectures; I do special tours, special exhibits, behind the scenes tours, re-enactors. We did free days and half-price days. We stayed away from coming in and listening to lectures."

THE ATARI VIRTUAL MUSEUM

BASIC DESCRIPTION OF THE ATARI VIRTUAL MUSEUM

The Atari Virtual Museum is based on the guerilla history efforts of one individual, Curt Vendel, who doggedly pursued and built the virtual museum, mostly as a private hobby. Currently, this virtual museum registers about 30,000 hits per month. The Museum offers images and documents relating the history of Atari, its products, executives and corporate lore.

The Museum's founder Curt Vendel, when asked why he started the Museum, said simply, "Some people collect stamps. I collect Atari stuff."

The Museum grew out of a bulletin board that Curt maintained in the late 1980s. Curt took a break from 1990 to 1994 and then started posting to the bulletin board again in 1994 and started the website in 1997.

MORE THAN PLAYING GAMES

In addition to an extensive collection featuring Atari's premier role in the video-game industry, the Atari Virtual Museum has information on Atari's role in other industries, such as interactive laser disks and telephones.

Curt notes that the Museum includes a document archive of "literally everything Atari, including commercials, photographs, PDF scans of memos of people being fired, company reports."

The Museum not only provides a window on the historic development of Atari products but on the inner dynamics of company decision-making. Curt was dogged in his pursuit of company history and memorabilia. His explanation is a kind of 101-course on guerilla history. The tactics can be used by any history aficionado, and by local historical societies and others interested in the raw material of history and its presentation.

He explains, "As the company changed hands they kept throwing things out. I would go out to the offices and I would go out and take everything out of the dumpsters. And over the years, I would do this and get studies and documents. I got production numbers and prices. I have been doing this for 21 years; this was my own guerilla historian effort and Atari did not have anything to do with it. There was nothing they could do – what was there it was in the public domain. I was contacted by former Atari people and they would say to me, 'I got stuff in my garage. Do you want it?' People would send me the stuff and I would pay the shipping. It has been good. There were times I got documents and blueprints that are pieces of history that are vanishing before your eyes."

VISITORS TO THE SITE

Frequent visitors to the museum site include "the nostalgia-conscious, others who are looking to understand test technology, others who are collecting old games and old computers and students, technology journalists, and tech companies." Users tend to be driven by a mixture of nostalgia and research.

MARKETING

The Atari Virtual Museum does little direct marketing but it makes itself known in the world of computer history through its collection, research and information activities. In addition, Curt does attend vintage computer shows, which are the main meeting venues for the computer history world.

"I go out to vintage computer shows – they cut me a break since I am not a vendor. There is the vintage computer festival; they have the east-coast one in the summer and the west-coast one is in the fall. Also some kind of video game shows are always going on all over the country."

Curt also makes himself known to major websites in the computer history world such as vintage-computer.org and computerhistory.org. In addition, Curt (a computer engineer in his non-guerilla historian roles) works as a consultant and designer for Atari, which still employs hundreds of people.

ADVICE

"It is all a matter of patience and really sitting down. A lot of people are into collecting hardware and games but I think the most valuable thing is paperwork that tells you everything from the inside out. You can find minutes and meeting notes and it reveals a lot of important clues and raises questions. And you can then find other documents (relating to the original ones) and that will give you answers. The best sources are people who worked for the company. It started out with me tracking down the known people in Atari and politely contacting them. The paperwork started coming in as more and more names came up. Take the time, dial those numbers and hope that you will find the right person. Most Atari people stayed in California so I could track them down. Keep going at it and eventually it pays off."

IMPLICATIONS OF THE ATARI VIRTUAL MUSEUM FOR OTHERS

The Atari Virtual Museum shows how a determined individual can – with a little grit and determination, and love of a subject – just go out and create a museum from scratch. History is in corners and crevices, in attics and junkyards and dustbins. The internet gives local historians like Curt an avenue to pursue grassroots history. It is an approach that can be successful for many small historical societies, nascent museums, struggling historic sites or – indeed – any organization or individual without much money to invest but with a great deal of enthusiasm.

THE KANSAS STATE HISTORICAL SOCIETY

BASIC DESCRIPTION OF THE KANSAS STATE HISTORICAL SOCIETY

The Kansas State Historical Society, with headquarters in Topeka, is a state agency with 95 full-time employees that preserves and promotes Kansas historic heritage. We spoke with Bobbie Athon, Director of Marketing and Communications for the Kansas State Historical Society.

The Society maintains 16 state historic sites in Kansas, including Fort Riley, the first territorial capital, the Kansas Museum of History, the Native American Heritage Museum, several former Native-American missions, and many other sites. The Society is also the trustee of the state archives, and maintains the state preservation office and an archeology division. The most recent addition to the state's roster of historic sites is the former home of Pulitzer Prize–winning newspaperman William Ellen White, publisher and editor of the *Imporia Gazzette*, and friend of Theodore Roosevelt.

The Society was founded as a private organization in 1875 by a group of Kansas newspaper editors and publishers; it was directed by a 99-member board. A few years later, the State of Kansas made the Society a trustee of the state's records, and for the remainder of the 19th and 20th centuries the Society was a mixed public-private organization. In 2001, the State Legislature officially made it a state agency. Its website is at www.kshs.org.

BUDGET & SITE ADMISSIONS

The Society has a $6-million budget and this is supplemented by about $120,000 in fees from admissions. The Society's small $50,000 marketing budget is supplemented by the admissions receipts.

The Kansas Historical Society's 16 sites get more than two million visitors per year. About a third of all visitors are school students, another third are local Kansans, mostly from the Kansas City/Lawrence/Topeka area, while another third are tourists and travelers, many of whom are from out of state. The flagship Kansas Museum of History gets about 100,000 visitors per year.

RESEARCH CENTER & DIGITIZATION OF ARCHIVES

In addition to its historic sites, state archives and archeological activities, the Society maintains a research center that "contains copies of nearly every newspaper published in the state, that goes prior to statehood," says Ms Athon. "We also have participated in a website called TerritorialKansasOnline.org, on which we put digital images of photographs, letters, and documents relating to the 'Bloody Kansas' 1854-1861 period. This was done in conjunction with the University of Kansas."

The site has thousands of items, including scanned letters from famous abolitionist John Brown. About 80% of the materials came from the Kansas State Historical Society and about 20% came from the University of Kansas. The two organizations had jointly applied for and won an IMLS grant to fund the project. The site is housed on the server of the University of Kansas. The grant had only a small amount set aside for marketing the site.

In addition to the historic documents, the site has lesson plans and other resources for teachers of American history. "Our museums and sites try to focus on the school audience and work with the state department of education," says Athon.

The Society also uses its publications to reach out to the school audience.

"We have a publication for fourth through sixth graders, this is when they cover Kansas history in school. It is called *Kaleidoscope*. It is just $7 per year for the subscription. It goes to Society members with children. Basic members receive *Kansas Heritage*, a quarterly magazine and they also receive *Kansas History* – a journal."

REACH OUT TO MEMBERSHIP

The Society has 4,000 members; they pay $40 annually for a basic membership and it gives them the two basic publications. The fee is $50 for family membership and they receive *Kaleidoscope* as well as the two other publications. Members receive free admission to all of the state historic sites.

RELATIONS WITH LOCAL KANSAS HISTORICAL SOCIETIES

Kansas has about 300 local historical societies. The Kansas State Historical Society has had a kind of unofficial relationship with them. "We have an unofficial relationship, "explains Athon. "In times past we have had programs to help them with their exhibits or given other types of assistance. But we do not do that any more. We have had many cutbacks in our staff."

HISTORICAL TOURISM

"We work closely with the state tourism office and we participate with them in programs; they host different conferences and we try to participate in them. The conferences are aimed at the travel industry in Kansas."

RESULTS OF RECENT MARKET RESEARCH STUDY

The Society just completed a market research study to try to understand its customers' needs better. The organization hired BBC Research of Denver and gave the firm an (approximately) $50,000 contract to study customer needs. The firm conducted focus groups, intercept surveys at major sites, and a telephone survey. The Society was pleased with the knowledge it gained and Athon notes that, "It helped us to understand what people know about us and don't know about us. I would recommend it to other agencies - the difficult part is acting on the information that you gain. That is the important part of it."

THE COMPUTER HISTORY MUSEUM

BASIC DESCRIPTION OF THE COMPUTER HISTORY MUSEUM

The Computer History Museum, located in Mountain View, California, was founded 25 years ago by Gordon Bell, Glenn Bell and Olsen, engineers for Digital Equipment Corporation. We spoke with Steven Brewster, Director of Marketing and Communications for the Computer History Museum.

The Museum opened in 1979 as part of a lobby atrium in a new office building that computer giant DEC had purchased from RCA. By the early 1980s the Museum had outgrown its lobby atrium roots and moved its now extensive collection to Boston, where it remained until 1996. The Museum's original founders grew somewhat disenchanted with the Museum's evolution in the direction of a children-oriented museum, and decided to change direction. The Museum moved to a temporary space in Silicon Valley and later bought a 120,000-square-foot building that had been home to the sales and marketing division of Silicon Graphics.

In order to pay for the building and build out the space, the Museum has embarked on a $100-million capital campaign, almost all of which it intends to raise through private donations. Thus far, according to Brewster, the Museum is "halfway there."

What is most interesting about the capital campaign is that the Museum has managed to raise $50 million even though it is not currently open to the public. Although the Museum maintains a web presence, arranges private viewings, raises funds, and builds its collection – it will not formally open again to the public until 2009. The Museum does open Wednesdays, Fridays and Saturdays for tours, and will open at other times for pre-arranged tours, but it will not fully function as a public museum for another four years.

The Museum raises considerable revenue from renting out its space for special events and it is a much sought-after venue for events in the computer industry. "Google had a huge holiday party here," said Brewster, "and we have four to five social events in the Museum every week."

MARKETING SPECIFIC EXHIBITS

The Museum is working with Van Sickle & Orlleri, a renowned exhibit-consulting firm that also worked on the Seattle Experience Music Project. Currently, the Museum has two exhibits up and running. The first is called the 'Visible Storage Exhibits', which encompasses about one tenth of the Museum's overall collection, and it traces the beginnings of computing (going back to the abacus) to supercomputing.

The second is called 'Innovation 101', and looks at the creative process. A third and entirely new exhibit will be dubbed 'Mastering the Game', a history of chess software. This exhibit, which will open in July, will feature guest speakers from IBM, as well as a chess tournament, and other popular features.

"We are going to target chess clubs and kids, and definitely we are going to be targeting engineers in software companies as well," says Brewster.

LECTURES & SPECIAL EVENTS

Brewster notes that there is a close association between the lectures and special events staged by the Museum and requests for tours and attendance.

He explains, "Basically the way we have been able to attract people is through the tremendous media coverage that we get for our lectures and special events, and we will then prompt people to come to other special events (or to the Museum itself through tours). We have a large lecture series that attracts many very capable people. We have had Bill Gates, for example – 400 or 500 people will come in for a lecture here. Our lecture series is a wonderful marketing tool. And that is now the most important thing – how can we engage the public through our special programs. The public programs allow the public to hear and talk to the computing greats."

GIFT SHOP

The Museum runs a small gift shop mostly stocked with logo items and computer books.

WEB PRESENCE

As might be expected of a computer museum, Brewster thinks that the Museum's web presence is very important and a great deal of thought has been given to the presentation of the Museum on the web.

"It is very important – if you go to Google we are the first thing that shows up on the search for computer history. We will be the first stop for people who are researching computer-industry history. Everything you see at the museum will be online so you can take a cybertour and we have streaming video and audio of the lectures after they happen."

The Museum also positions its experts to play a role in research conducted by other institutions by being open to questions from the public. Brewster believes it is important to maintain the Museum's image as computer-history experts and, while the Museum does charge for industry-specific research, it will also answer many questions gratis. The Museum very much values its image as a 'first stop' for computer-history research and views its web presence, and access to its experts and exhibits, as part of this important image.

Currently, a 'good portion' of the hits on the Museum's website come from academic institutions worldwide, especially from those countries with ample computer industries, such as South Korea or Switzerland.

Links with the academic world build the Museum's reputation, and expand its attendance base. "We are linked in with a lot of different schools here and abroad. We share information – through our research and curatorial staff. We don't go out and make the contacts, the contacts are already there. We deal with the people who made the history – they want to preserve their legacy – they make sure we have the right documentation and that we have the oral history recorded.

The Museum's entire collection is "pretty much entirely donated," says Brewster and involvement with trustees, board members, donors and associates creates not just a steady stream of support for the museum, – in terms of additions to the collection and funds – but also a network through which to market.

COOPERATION WITH INDUSTRY ASSOCIATIONS

The Museum does not have to market too aggressively since the computer industry's many associations tend to come to it. "We are involved in a long list of associations – IEEE, ACM – they come to us and want to be part of us," says Brewster. "Locally we are linked in with the Silicon Valley Concierge Association – they will send them to us."

The Museum also intends to aggressively enhance its online presence by developing a cybermuseum by 2009. Says Brewster: "We will also have online by 2009 a complete cybermuseum. Now we have just highlights. We will also have a research library – part of it – for limited use by the public, though the full parameters have not been defined yet."

ADVICE TO OTHER MARKETERS

"I would say when you are in the nascent stages of building a museum you should be extremely involved with your trustees and advisory board. Some museums overlook their expertise; they have built in networks that can be engaged at a moment's notice."

The website is at www.computerhistory.org.

THE MUSEUM OF AMERICAN FINANCIAL HISTORY

BASIC DESCRIPTION OF THE MUSEUM OF AMERICAN FINANCIAL HISTORY

The Museum of American Financial History is located in the John D Rockefeller building in lower Manhattan in New York City. The Museum's exhibits are in the building's lobby, while its offices and library are in office space on higher floors. The Museum currently occupies 6,000 square feet but is moving to a 21,000 square foot space (also in lower Manhattan) in 2006. The Museum has a small staff of three: an executive director, a marketing specialist, and an education director. In addition, the Museum has volunteers and several part-timers who staff the museum shop, keep the books and do other tasks. We spoke with Kristin Aguilera, Communications Director of the Museum of American Financial History.

The Museum of American Financial History was founded in 1988, in many ways as a response to the great stock market crash of 1987. The Museum was founded by John Herzog who, at the time of the crash, was an executive with a major securities firm.

"He realized that no one was saving Wall Street's history and that it was particularly important. He was a long time collector of documents of American financial history – dating back to the 18th century. He had a large personal collection and he realized that no institution was saving this history, so he donated his collection to found the museum," explains Aguilera."

In that collection of about 5,000 to 6,000 financial documents, largely 18th-century material, were many of the founding financial documents of the United States. "We have the first bond issue of the United States issued to George Washington and signed by him," says Aguilera, "Washington was one of the first purchasers of the first bond issue; this is the first use of the dollar sign on a federal document in the United States. And we have a number of letters and documents pertaining to Alexander Hamilton. We have letters written by him to the Bank of New York, actually asking for support for the first bond issue which he created."

The Museum now has more than 10,000 items including photographs, historic stocks and bonds, currency, stock tickers and other Wall Street technology, and other items of historic interest.

The Museum also maintains a research library which houses, among other items, the entire archive of the old American Bank Company, described by Aguilera as "The company that engraved and printed just about all of the stocks and bonds in our country. It went bankrupt in the 1990s but was founded in the civil war. We have their order books – some of the first stock and bond issues."

IMPACT OF THE EVENTS OF 9/11 ON MUSEUM ATTENDANCE

The Museum is located just a few blocks from the World Trade Center site, destroyed in the terrorist attacks of September 11, 2001. As a result of the attacks, the economy of downtown Manhattan where the Museum is located, turned down sharply. Poor air quality from the vast amounts of residue that poured into the atmosphere, the need to clear debris and identify victims, and a psychological aversion to pursuing pleasurable activities in the area of such a national tragedy, all led to sharp declines in attendance at the Museum of American Financial History, and other museums and cultural institutions in lower Manhattan. Prior to the events of 9/11 the Museum drew 30,000 visitors annually. This fell off drastically after 9/11, but the Museum has been able to restore attendance to approximately 20,000 or about two-thirds of pre-9/11 levels.

REACH OUT TO STUDENTS

About 40% of the visitors to the Museum are students, and the institution maintains a full-time educator to cater to student groups. The Museum's financial education program starts with fifth graders and goes up through to adult education. Investment clubs are a favorite marketing target, along with students who play a popular Wall Street investment game designed to teach them the main elements of successful investing.

"We are doing a lot with financial literacy and teaching people how to make wise investment decisions," explains Aguilera. "You could have a class on basic finance, or how to start a small business, or there can be something tied to an exhibit."

EXHIBITS

Current exhibits include 'Making Money: Bank Note Engraving and the Fight Against Counterfeiting', put up in conjunction with the Secret Service and the Department of the Treasury.

The Museum tries to make its exhibits interactive, especially since students constitute such a large share of its attendance base. "We have sample counterfeit notes, and we have a station where people can examine the most modern notes to be able to recognize all of the security features in the current US currency so you do not get stuck with a counterfeit. They actually brought an Iraqi *dinar* that had been bleached out and printed as US currency; this is the current counterfeiting strategy in Iraq, the paper has the right feel and the right size."

Another new exhibit is called 'Survival of the Fittest: the Evolution of the Dow Jones Industrial Average.' "It is based on original research on tracing the Dow. Eleven of the 12 that were the original companies that started the Dow are still in existence today. Only US Leather does not still exist. All the others, many of them have changed names and changed hands, but they still exist."

MARKETING EFFORTS

The Museum buys ads in museum magazines such as *Museums New York* but tends to focus on grassroots public relations.

"All press releases we put on *Businesswire*. We do it through one of our board members who has an account. And I also have my own press contacts."

Aguilera always makes sure to invite many journalists to the parties that open new exhibits. "We were in *Barrons* last week," she beamed, referring to the well-known financial weekly.

"Last night we had a party and we invited press to attend that. How many journalists attended – 17 signed up – I would say that 10 came."

Typically the Museum, which charges just $2 for admission, is most busy in fall and spring. Before the attacks of 9/11 the Museum drew 30,000 visitors annually, but after the attacks the Museum had to close for a month and attendance plummeted.

THE MUSEUMS OF LOWER MANHATTAN MARKETING CAMPAIGN

As part of a federal-local effort to rebuild lower Manhattan after the attacks of 9/11, 15 museums in lower Manhattan received a $4.5-million grant from the Lower Manhattan Development Corporation. The grant was specifically to help these 15 museums with their marketing, and the campaign built with these funds has become known as the Museums of Lower Manhattan Marketing Campaign. What is interesting about the grant is that the entire grant is being spent on marketing, and cooperatively features all the museums, although particular ads may focus more on some museums than others. The funds will be spent over a four-year period and the first disbursements were made in 2004.

The grants have enabled the Museum and its partners to try new advertising approaches. One that they have found effective is advertising on the New York City subway.

"We have done a lot of transit ads which have been effective. I think it has something to do with there being such a captive audience and they are coming this way anyway. We did a campaign with the MTA – two for one admission if you show your metro card [a card that can be used to pay for subway trips in New York City]." The website is at nystartshere.org.

The Museum also found it useful to distribute brochures with maps showing the Museum's location, finding this a considerable aid in attracting walk-in traffic. The coalition also sponsored a fitness walk "basically trying to draw people downtown for something other than going to ground zero [the site of the attacks]" and also providing a nice way to introduce the walkers to lower Manhattan's 15 museums that participate in the joint marketing effort.

The Museum has also managed to attract quite a few foreign visitors, especially from Japan, and it tries to be picked up in domestic and foreign tour guides to New York City, as well as the local convention and tourism guides.

PARTNERSHIPS

As many museums have found, marketing partnerships with organizations in some way thematically related to the museum and its mission can be particularly rewarding. For the past two years, the Museum has received grants from the Securities Industry Association, which runs a well-known and popular stock-market game designed to introduce students to the world of investing. The Museum participates in this game by teaching students some basic investing concepts and participating in the awards ceremony and other facets of the stock-market game.

The Museum uses the $10,000 annual grant from the Securities Industry Association to conduct a direct-mail campaign aimed at high-school students. Tour groups from high schools can view the Museum for a flat feel of only $50 per group. Aguilera notes, "That has been extremely successful – we have been booked solid with tour groups in the fall and spring. We have groups coming just about every day and we have about 8,000 visitors per year through these groups."

We asked whether the Museum targets high-school business teachers in its promotional mailings. Aguilera responded that, "We get a lot of math teachers. A lot of high schools do have business classes but not all of them, and we keep our own records of the teachers who visit us."

The Museum is able to obtain the lists directly from the New York City Board of Education. Currently, the mailings are sent to teachers within New York City's official city limits, since the Museum has reached its capacity, though when the Museum moves to a bigger space, it may broaden its mailings.

The Museum adjusts its in-Museum sales strategy. Since students have so much less money than the typical Wall-Street executives who make up another large block of attendees, the Museum rolls out a cart with low end items for sale. Like many Museums, its gift shop tends to focus on high-end items such as expensive prints and works of art used often to decorate executive offices. Carts rolled out into the gallery for students have less expensive items such as souvenirs like mugs, pens and T-shirts emblazoned with financial images. Other items include bags of shredded money and big pencils emblazoned with currencies.

The Museum has also benefited from cooperation with local schools of business.

Explains Aguilera: "We work with the NYU Stern School – we do really nice author events with some high-profile names. For example, we had Bob Rubens (Treasury Secretary in the Clinton Administration). We work with NYU on an ongoing basis. We have done some programming with Baruch (Business-oriented college of the City University of New York) with their financial journalism program. A lot of the schools do have tours and things here."

USE OF PR AGENCIES

The Museum does much of its own public relations work but also works through public relations and advertising agencies Dan Klores Communications, and the advertising agency Bandujo Donker & Company.

ADVICE

"What I would say is most effective here; PR is extremely important. We get a lot of calls from the press looking for images to run with their stories, or looking for us to provide some fact checking for them. Our magazine actually predates the museum. We try to make sure that we are as helpful as possible and hopefully they pay you back by coming to your events and writing you up. Bend over backwards for them and then go back to them and ask them to write you up when you have a new exhibit. I have found that it is more effective to do your own PR. I think people are more receptive for that since they know that you will help them out when they need some research help with something."

THE ATLANTA HISTORY CENTER

BASIC DESCRIPTION OF THE ATLANTA HISTORY CENTER

The Atlanta History Center was founded in 1926 as the Atlanta Historical Society, initially meeting in "people's homes and basements" to devise ways to preserve Atlanta's rich history.

The History Center as it is known today began to truly take shape when, in 1966, the organization purchased the Swan House, a local landmark originally constructed in 1928 and designed by the renowned architect Phillip Trammel Sheutz. The Swan House and its surrounding grounds became the basis for an expanding center that now comprises a 33-acre 'campus'. In 1990 the Atlanta Historical Society changed its name for branding purposes and in 2004 the Center completed a major $5.4-million renovation of the Swan House. We spoke with Hillary Hardwick, Director of Marketing Communications for The Atlanta History Center.

The Atlanta History Center uses the Swan House and related adjacent properties to exhibit and illustrate themes in Atlanta history. The Swan House itself is presented as a representation of upscale Atlanta life in the 1920s, complete with much of the original furniture and furnishings. The Swan House's wood paneled library, butler's pantry, family and formal-dining rooms, and other features illustrate the lives of well-heeled Atlantans in the roaring 20s.

In addition to the Swan House itself, the 33-acre campus includes the James Kenan Research Center and Archives; the Archives cover Atlanta and general southern history, and it has become a noted information center for Atlantans and for scholars of southern life. It is one of the first stops for researchers on local genealogy and information on old homes in Atlanta. The Center gets more than 150,000 visitors annually.

MEMBERSHIP COST & BENEFITS

The Atlanta History Center has 6,000 members; the Center charges $75 for a family membership, $25 for students and teachers, $50 for other individual memberships, and $65 for a dual membership. Most members live in the Atlanta metropolitan area. One-day admission is $12 for adults, $7 for kids aged between four and 12 years of age, $10 for seniors and students, and it is free for children aged three and under.

Members receive free entry and passes for guests, and they are the first to receive notification for lecture series' and other events, as well as discounted rates to events. They also get first crack at the tickets and are offered the opportunity to buy before tickets are sold to the general public. The Center's events are often well attended and Hardwick feels that one of the key attractions of membership is this feature that allows members to purchase event tickets before they are made available to the general public.

EVENTS MARKETING

The Center uses events marketing as a kind of Trojan horse to pull people to the Swan House, showing them different faces of Atlanta history and keeping them coming back. One of its most important events is an annual conference/concert called 'Nothin' but the Blues'. The Center collaborates with Eric King, co-owner of Blind Willies, a local blues club. "We have been working with Eric for seven years," says Hardwick, "and the concert series has grown from one night to two nights." The second night repeats the first night's performance for a largely new audience.

The concert is on the first Thursday and Friday of February, March, April, and May. Hardwick says that a broad range of ticket prices allows a broad range of people to attend. The average price for non-members is $90 for the entire concert series, and $70 for members. The concerts are held indoors.

Hardwick emphasizes that the series stays true to its blues roots and brings listeners true blues performances from the best blues musicians

"We bring in the heritage blues musicians; it really is educational. We were recently awarded by the WC Handy Blues Foundation (based in Memphis) and they recognize blues performers for top CD sales. They are the blues experts and they gave us an award called the 'Keepin' the Blues Alive' award. This year we have sold out every concert so far and we can seat 400 in one night."

The grounds also comprise the 1845 Tullie Smith Farm, an authentic working 1840-style farmhouse that once produced a mix of cotton and vegetables. "The farm has seven outbuildings associated with it and we do a lot of living history out at the farm," explains Hardwick. "We have a blacksmith shop and blacksmithing demonstrations. We have a barn, though we currently do not have any farm animals because of restoration. However we have had and will again have 'sheep to shawl' which shows the whole shearing process. Kids come in and they shear our sheep."

The Atlanta History Center also has seven different gardens on its grounds. One is a quarry garden that is actually in the site of an abandoned rock quarry, and it shows plants that were native to pre-settlement Georgia. Another is a garden showing heirloom plants that would have been used in the 19th century.

To publicize events and attractions, The Atlanta History Center relies on well-placed ads in local publications and extensive public relations. "I do not have much advertising budget. A lot is done through grassroots and public relations. The advertising we do goes into tourism magazines locally like *Atlanta Now*."

DIMENSIONS OF THE STAFF

The Atlanta History Center has over 80 full-time staff, and also draws on a pool of about over 300 volunteers. The Center has been particularly successful in attracting volunteers and they play a wide range of rolls.

"We have administrative volunteers, we have volunteers who give tours in the gallery, those who usher for our lecture series and blues series. They come in through word of mouth. We do volunteer orientations and when we hold the orientations we notify the newspapers."

INCREASING ATTENDANCE

Many historical attractions nationwide have lost attendance in recent years, but attendance has been increasing at the Atlanta History Center.

"I think there are a couple of different reasons," speculates Hardwick, "one is the Swan House Restoration. We got some really great publicity on that. We were able to add on five rooms for touring. The Swan House is traditionally the most photographed landmark in Atlanta.

Another reason our attendance has continued to increase is that we have the Atlanta History Museum. This houses four permanent exhibitions that cover the history of Atlanta from 1836 to the present day. And then we have an exhibit called *Turning Point: the American Civil War*. We market that through general brochures and through the visitors' center, through the convention and visitors' bureau that is one of our main attractions. It is one of the largest civil-war exhibitions in the southeast."

WEB MARKETING STRATEGY

The Center personalized its website to enable visitors to the site to plan their visit from the website. Hardwick explains: "We are starting to get more into web marketing. We just launched a new website in January of this year. It is much more interactive and easier to navigate [than the old site]. We have a feature that allows you to plan your visit on our website. You can go in and put in the dates that you are gong to be in and you check your interest area, so it will pull up any events or lectures or exhibits or family programs that are occurring during their visit and that correlate to their interests. It is interest-driven on behalf of the visitor. We have a section on the website that says 'Plan your Visit'. You can sign up for events. We do not have the ability to do onsite ticket purchase but that is what we will do next." The website is at www.atlantahistorycenter.com.

In addition to its revised website, the Center has just started to use email marketing.

"We just last week sent out our first email campaign to our members to have people opt in or opt out and we will send out an e-newsletter the last week of every month. It is written in-house and it mirrors exactly what out website looks like. Anyone who goes on the website can sign up for our e-newsletter. What I can do once the campaign rolls out is that I can see what people are clicking on so I will be able to do more targeted campaigns in the future. Our print newsletter is strictly members but our e-newsletter we are happy to send to anyone who wants it."

THE BLOCKBUSTER LECTURE AS MARKETING TOOL

Hardwick believes that the blockbuster lecture has helped the Center to spread its name and generate much repeat business. Although this strategy may be risky for smaller organizations, the Atlanta History Center has prospered by presenting major authors such as David McCullough and other well-known figures as guest lecturers. The Center charges $7 to non-members and $5 for members, and typically draws a sold out audience.

Hardwick has found that the local public broadcasting station is a good venue to advertise lectures, and the Center pays about $1,500 for about two weeks' of broadcast spots on the local area PBS Atlanta affiliate. The lectures are also supported by direct-mail efforts aimed mostly at members, as well as listings in local newspapers and guides.

EXHIBITS WITH AN INTERACTIVE TOUCH

The goal of good history marketing is always to present the old in a new and interesting way. The Atlanta History Center accomplishes this by changing its traveling exhibits every three or four months, and including interactive features that draw in those who may not have considered themselves history buffs.

Hardwick describes a current exhibit: "'V is for Victory – Georgia Remembers WWII', that is an exhibit that the history center put together from our collection – it will be up for 13 months. It is a tribute to the WWII generation and we have a program called 'WWII Remembrance Day'. Visitors come in and we have WWII jeeps and living-history interpreters. We have people talking about what combat would have been like, both historians and actual veterans. The biggest part of that day is that families can come in and talk about WWII veterans. They have tables set up with their letters home, their photographs, uniforms, and memorabilia. We have veterans from the WWII Round Table in Atlanta. The exhibits open and you get one to two weeks of great publicity but to keep that constant I truly believe it takes interactive programming – to keep people coming back. On Remembrance Day they can come in and hold a weapon and see how heavy it is. In many museums you get the feeling that you really can't touch anything and we try to do the opposite here. In our Metropolitan Frontiers we have a little symbol – it is little magnifying glass that says AHC – and this is a sign that they can touch the object."

PARTNERSHIPS

With a limited marketing budget, Hardwick feels it is useful to enter into cross-marketing arrangements with other local cultural institutions.

She tells about a recent joint venture, "Our local theater group called the Alliance Theater had a play called *Crown*, and they focused on what do hats mean in the African-American family. They had stuff in our member newsletter and they included us in theirs. We had onsite presence at the openings of their plays and we did advertising in their playbills and all that was free – it was just a cross promotional partnership. It makes senses – the audiences are good matches – theaters and museums."

MAJOR RENOVATIONS

The Atlanta History Center recently completed its renovations of the Swan House and it now undertaking similarly bold renovations on its Museum, which is getting a three-story addition. The first story will house a centennial exhibit of the 1996 Atlanta Olympic Games. A lower level will be an open 6,000-foot gallery space to bring in big blockbuster exhibitions from the outside. The highest floor will house an interactive sports center, where kids will be able to sample Olympic sports. The Museum will house interactive exhibits for kayaking, archery, and perhaps the long jump. The exhibits will allow kids to test their skills and they will be issued a card that will tell them how they performed at the end of the day.

ADDITIONAL SOURCES OF REVENUE

The Atlanta History Center rents out the Swan House for weddings and other special events such as birthdays, corporate presentations, bat mitzvahs and other such events. The Center's ample grounds can be rented for picnics and barbecues, and the museum is rented out for two-hour periods for special receptions and events.

The Center also features two theaters and two restaurants, one that is a 1950s-style soda shop, and another, an elegant upscale restaurant – the Swan Coach House Restaurant – housed in the actual coach house of the estate.

FOR THE FUTURE

In August of 2004 The Atlanta History Center acquired the Margaret Mitchell Site and Museum; Margaret Mitchell was the author of *Gone With the Wind*. The site attracts many international visitors and the Center is experiencing an upsurge in international visitors as a result of the acquisition. The Center will focus on cross-pollinating visitors to the Swan House with those at the Margaret Mitchell Site and Museum, as well as pressing forward with its Museum renovations.

VANDERBILT UNIVERSITY LIBRARY, THE DENVER PUBLIC LIBRARY & THE EVANSVILLE PUBLIC LIBRARY

THE ROLE OF THE LIBRARY IN HISTORIC PRESERVATION

Increasingly, the Nation's public libraries are taking the initiative to present historic documents, photographs, manuscripts, and artifacts to the general public. Public libraries have always played this role, but the emergence of digital libraries and searching technologies have put public libraries in the forefront of such efforts. Interestingly, and perhaps surprisingly, public libraries are in many ways further along than academic and special libraries in their efforts to market their digital collections. Academic libraries often have the most impressive digital collections, and a few major research libraries can count on massive financial support to digitize and market their collections. However, the utilization of these collections, at least so far, has been somewhat disappointing. Public libraries, on the other hand, have been pressured by patrons to make their historic collections more accessible, and to develop new collections built around local needs. In the following section we take a look at two public libraries that have developed useful approaches to making their history collections more accessible to the public

In academic circles, the digitization of images, in art, photography, archeology, architecture, film, television and theater, has perhaps created the most enthusiasm, or at least precipitated the most usage. Digitization efforts have brought to life historic collections of photographs, posters, newsreels and film footage. We look briefly at one of the best known such efforts, that of Vanderbilt University.

The Denver Public Library has a Central Library and 22 branches, all serving the city of Denver's approximately 600,000 citizens. The overall library budget in 2005 was $28 million. We spoke with Jo Haight Sarling, Director of Access and Technology Services of the Denver Public Library.

The Library has been heavily involved in the digitization of its special collections.

"We have been digitizing a collection of photographs in our western history department – old photographs of the West, local photographs going back to the 1800s, such as practically every train that has come out West, Indian photographs, etc. These photos have been digitized and enhanced in such a way that in our building you can access them with special software that allows you to digitally enhance the photo and zoom in on it. You can have access to these through our website. They are all cataloged and you can access them with a keyword like "velvet." A search on "velvet" would get pictures of women in velvet ball gowns, and pictures of houses in Georgetown (a silver mining town) with velvet flocked wallpaper. We continue to digitize these and we are beginning to digitize art that we own."

We asked Sarling if the Library was cooperating with any major academic research libraries in the area.

"No, we do this on our own," she says. "We have a very large camera that is suspended from the ceiling and it is almost the size of a queen-size bed. We use this for articles and maps. We have some very rare maps and other pieces of our western history collection such as mining prospectuses or invitations to balls."

The Library supports its digitization effort through grants and by selling reproductions of images to the public. Images are sold in the library itself, and also from the Library website. Typical prices for an 8x10 inch photograph on a glossy or map finish is about $19 while a 16x20 inch signed art map might cost about $46, and a 40x50 inch architectural drawing or map might command $140. Prices depend on the size, quality and type of finish. The Library also sells rights to media outlets to publish photographs and other aspects of its collection.

The Library also sells items emblazoned with images; some popular items are postcards, journals, lunch boxes, mouse pads, T-shirts, sweat shirts, coffee mugs, and tote bags.

"We have a few of these things in the library itself in the coffee shop and in the Western History Department," says Sarling.

CAPTURING LOCAL HISTORY AT THE EVANSVILLE PUBLIC LIBRARY

The Evansville, Indiana Public Library has cleverly developed local databases based on available public records and local special collections. The Library has four heavily used, locally developed databases that track the history and genealogy of the Evansville community. The first is a database of local obituaries developed by a local undertaker – Mr. Browning – who has been in the community for many years. We spoke with Mr. Mike Abarary, Associate Director of Floor Support Services for the Evansville Public Library.

"It is heavily used for genealogy, and it is used worldwide," says Abaray. The second is a database of press clippings from a now defunct Evansville newspaper – the Evansville Press – which gave the Evansville Public library its morgue, a database of past issues and other materials related to the newspaper and the community. A third database, also developed by the mortician Mr Browning, is called the Browning People Studies. It contains 520,000 cards filled with information about people from Evansville, including brief biographical information from newspapers, marriage announcements and licenses, high school yearbooks, church records, press clippings and other publicly available information about Evansville residents. It also includes information about individuals who have recently left Evansville such as retirees in Florida. A fourth database, Evansville Electronic Books, has books about local history that are no longer under copyright.

The databases are linked and can be searched jointly through WebFeat, the Library's federated search system, which it has had in place for about a year.

"It has been real good and our database's usage has really taken off because of the federated searching," enthuses Abaray. "All the databases in the catalog can be searched at one time if you want to. You can search by category or you can also search the individual databases as well. You are validated as you go into it and you simply put in your search; you can limit by language or date – it is relatively simple and easy to use. It is great for our customers, many of whom want ten articles for a high school paper (and not something much more elaborate.) But we think it also has a lot of flexibility. You are searching 61 databases plus the catalog at the same time. They do all the work. It was easy to implement. WebFeat does all the work for us – we don't have the staff to do it in house."

VANDERBILT UNIVERSITY DIGITIZED NEWS BROADCAST ARCHIVE

The Library is currently in the midst of a major strategic planning overhaul, one aspect of which is its plan to digitize aspect of its special collections. The Library' has various digital initiatives underway but its main initiative is to digitize the Vanderbilt television news archive. The Archive encompasses broadcast United States national news from 1968 onward and includes extensive footage from the national news broadcasts of ABC, CBS, and NBC; the archive added CNN in 1995 and Fox News in 2004. In addition to national daily news broadcasts, the collection includes coverage of special events, such as major speeches, political conventions and significant news conferences, as well as complete 24 hour coverage for about a week or two of the events of 9/11.

The networks maintain copyright to the broadcasts but the index to them is available on the web. The digitization project supplements Vanderbilt's existing videotape loan service from the archive, requests for which can be initiated through the Vanderbilt library web site.

The Library recently launched a subscription service for K-12 educational institutions through which it provides streaming video access to the CNN portion of the collection. End users can view it through a streaming media player but cannot save it. "Our agreement with CNN requires that it (the streaming video footage) be at least three days old." Only CNN has granted Vanderbilt the rights to use its footage in this fashion with the proviso that, as Breeding explains: "The streaming service is exclusively for educational users." However, the Vanderbilt video lending service, based on the same collection, "is for commercial use and the general public as well as for educational purposes." Consequently, the Library will continue its videotape loan program even after it digitizes the complete national broadcast news archive. Copyright law protects the traditional video access method but does not give Vanderbilt rights to stream video from the major networks.

The Library has already digitized all of its CNN footage and has started on the rest of its collection. Overall, it is about two fifths of the way through the digitization process and has digitized broadcasts through 1980 (as well as all of the CNN broadcasts). The Library is currently digitizing about 100 broadcasts per day.

In order to digitize the video collection, Vanderbilt developed its own workstation solution; it funded this hardware/software project through a National Science Foundation (NSF) grant. The workstation is crafted by melding together various pre-existing software and hardware components; the Library also obtained local grants to produce a dozen such workstations from the template developed with the NSF grant. For the most part, Vanderbilt developers used commercially available software such as Moviemaker and combined them with locally written Pearl scripts.

OTHER REPORTS FROM PRIMARY RESEARCH GROUP INC.

RETIREMENT LOCATION PLANS OF AMERICANS AGED 50 AND OVER
PRICE: $495

This report looks at the retirement plans of maturing Americans. The report measures the level of interest in retiring to the following destinations (presenting unique data sets for each state cited): Florida, California, Texas, Arizona, North Carolina, Nevada, Pennsylvania, New Jersey, Georgia, Virginia, and Washington State. The report also measures current and expected interest in time-shares, gated communities, communities that restrict children, views on retirement overseas, and plans to retire to move to new locations upon retirement.

GAMBLING HABITS OF AMERICANS AGED 50 AND OVER
PRICE: $795   APRIL 2005

This report gives extensive data on the demographic characteristics of Americans who gamble, where they gamble, where they intend to gamble in the future, and how much they spend, not just on gambling but on food, lodging and entertainment as well. Presents data on how Americans view the moral appropriateness of gambling, and whether they have gambled in casinos in Las Vegas, Reno, and Atlantic City or on Indian reservations. The report tells you whether gamblers feel that they lost or won money and how much they feel that they won or lost. Presents data on the demographics of internet gambling, use of state lotteries, blackjack, poker, roulette, betting on horse racing, betting on college sports, and betting on professional sports. More than 250 tables of data paint a picture of the gambling habits of Americans aged 50 and over.

DOMESTIC TRAVEL AND VACATION PLANS OF AMERICANS AGED 50 AND OVER
PRICE: $795   APRIL 2005

This report presents extensive demographic data on interest in travel to many specific destinations including: Southern California; Central/Northern California; the Napa Valley; Yosemite National Park; Miami, Florida; Fort Lauderdale, Florida; Key West, Florida; Tampa, Florida; North Carolina; Maine; Idaho; Montana; Crater Lake, Oregon; Seattle, Washington; Virginia; Shenandoah Valley, Virginia; White Mountains; New Hampshire; Smokey Mountains; Tennessee; the Ozarks; Savanna, Georgia; Atlanta, Georgia; Phoenix, Arizona; Las Vegas, Nevada, Vail, Colorado; Cape May, New Jersey; Scottsdale, Arizona; Washington DC; New York City; Puerto Rico; and Hawaii.

The study also reports on travel habits and plans by bus, by train, by train via Amtrak, by air, by car, and by ship. Presents average spending on trips, demographic data on those interested in Elderhostel type trips, on 'singles' trips, and trips with grandchildren. This report can also be purchased in segments: $80 for data relating to any particular place or question.

FOREIGN TRAVEL AND VACATION PLANS OF AMERICANS AGED 50 AND OVER
PRICE: $995 APRIL 2005

The report presents 300 tables of data highlighting travel plans, with 13 tables of data devoted to each of the following destinations: Bermuda, the Bahamas, Jamaica, Puerto Rico, the Virgin Islands, St Martin, Trinidad, Mexico, Germany, Austria, Switzerland, the UK, Spain, Portugal, Ireland, Northern Italy, Southern Italy, Sweden, Denmark, Poland, the Czech Republic, Russia, New Zealand and Australia, South Africa, Morocco, Israel and Egypt, Brazil, Argentina, Japan, India, Thailand, Malaysia, Indonesia, South Korea, and Vietnam. The report also presents data on overseas travel plans over the next two years, spending on overseas travel, and use of internet travel sites. Buy the complete report or get data for your choice of ten countries of those listed for $300.

HOTEL AND MOTEL CHAINS: BRAND-NAME RECOGNITION & EVALUATION BY AMERICANS AGED 50 AND OVER
PRICE: $1,095 APRIL 2005

This report presents data on who has heard of, or stayed in, a broad range of hotel/motel chains with data broken out specifically for the following chains: Days Inn, Radissons, Hyatt, Marriott, Hilton, Hampton Inn, Ballys, Best Western, Camino Real, Budget Inn, Holiday Inn, Comfort Inn, Howard Johnson, Quality Inn, Residence Inn, Hotel 6, Ramada Inn, Carlton Hotels, Sleep Inn, Sheraton Hotels, Signature Inn, Super 8, Travel Lodge, Westin Hotels & Resorts, and Wyndham Hotels. Also presents data on use of Travelocity, Orbitz, Priceline, Hotwire, Hotels.com, Cheaphotels.com, and Discounthotels.com. Gives data on the mean number of rooms booked over the internet in the past two years, level of customer loyalty to hotels/motels, annual spending on hotels, high and low prices paid for rooms, and number of days spent in hotels and motels per year.

HOW AMERICANS AGED 50 AND OVER VIEW CRUISES AND CRUISE SHIP LINES
PRICE: $1,095 APRIL 2005

Gives data on the percentage of Americans who have taken a cruise and plan to take a cruise within the next three years. Gives spending data and breaks out data separately for those who have ever spent more than $1,500 per person for a cruise. Measures interest level in taking cruises to the following distinct destinations: Caribbean, Eastern Mediterranean, Western Mediterranean, Alaska Coastline, Greek Isles, South Pacific, Scandinavian Coast, the Mississippi River, the Danube, the Rhine, Australia/Great Barrier Reef, Arctic, or Antarctic.

LIBRARY REPORTS

BEST PRACTICES OF PUBLIC LIBRARY INFORMATION TECHNOLOGY DIRECTORS
Price: $65   FEBRUARY 2005
ISBN: 1-57440-073-8

This special report from Primary Research Group is based on exhaustive interviews with information technology directors and other critical staff involved in IT decision-making from the Princeton Public Library, the Minneapolis Public Library, the Boston Public Library, the Seattle Public Library, Cedar Rapids Public Library, San Francisco Public Library, the Denver Public Library, Evansville Public Library and the Santa Monica Public Library. The report – which is in an interview format and presents the views of the institutions cited above as well as Primary Research Group commentary – presents insights into the myriad of technology-related issues confronting today's public librarians, including issues involved with: internet filtering, workstation management and development, PC image roll out, equipment and vendor selection, database licensing, internet-access policies, automated book check-in and check-out systems, cataloging, and catalog enhancement, voice over IP, digitization of special collections, development of technology centers, wireless access, use of e-books, outsourcing, IT-staff training, virtual reference, and much more.

TRAINING COLLEGE STUDENTS IN INFORMATION LITERACY: PROFILES OF HOW COLLEGES TEACH THEIR STUDENTS TO USE ACADEMIC LIBRARIES
PRICE: $69.50   JANUARY 2003
ISBN: 1-57440-059-2

This special report profiles how more than a dozen academic libraries are coping with the surge of web/database education requests. The report covers the development of online tutorials, distribution of teaching loads and levels of specialization among library staff, the perils of teaching library science to English 101 and Psychology 101 students, as well as advanced personalized tutorials for PhD candidates and professors. Among the specialized topics covered: How libraries are reaching out and teaching distance learners and how are they negotiating help from other college departments, such as academic computing and education, and from in-house instructional technology programmers. Other issues explored include the library-education efforts of consortiums and partnerships, use of knowledge-management and reference software for library training, the development of savvy library web pages and tutorials for training, and the thorny issue of negotiating training support from vendors.

CREATING THE VIRTUAL REFERENCE SERVICE
PRICE: $85.00   JANUARY 2003
ISBN: 1-57440-058-4

This report profiles the efforts of 15 academic, special, and public libraries to develop digital reference services. The aim of the study is to enable other libraries to benefit from their experience in deciding whether, and how, to develop a digital-reference service, how much time, money and other resources to spend on it, how to plan it, institute it and evaluate it. Let librarians – in their own words – tell you about their experiences with digital reference.

Among the libraries and other organizations profiled are: Pennsylvania State University, Syracuse University's Virtual Reference Desk, the Massachusetts Institute of Technology, Palomar College, The Library of Congress, the University of Florida, PA Librarian Live, the Douglas County Public Library, the Cleveland Public Library, Denver Public Library, OCLC, the New England Law Library Consortium, the Internet Public Library, Paradise Valley Community College, Yale University Law School, Oklahoma State University, Tutor.Com and Baruch College.

PRIVATE COLLEGE INFORMATION TECHNOLOGY BENCHMARKS
PRICE: $295   JANUARY 2003
ISBN: 1-57440-060-6

Private College Information Technology Benchmarks presents more than 650 tables and charts exploring the use of information technology by small- and medium-sized private colleges in the United States. The report covers both academic and administrative computing, and breaks out data by enrollment size and level of tuition charged. Sixteen private American colleges contributed data to the report.

LAW LIBRARY BENCHMARKS, 2004-05 EDITION
PRICE: $115   EXPECTED PUBLICATION DATE: AUGUST 2004
ISBN: 1-57440-070-3

Law Library Benchmarks presents data from more than 70 law libraries, including those of major law firms, law schools, government agencies and courthouses. Data is broken out by type of law library. Includes detailed data on: library dimensions and physical and 'e-traffic' to the library, trends in library staff size, salaries and budget, precise statistics on use of librarian time, spending trends in the library content budget, spending on specific types of legal information, such as state and local codes or legal journals, spending on databases and commercial online services, use of, and plans for, CD-ROM, parent-organization management's view of the future of the law library, assessment of library resources for analyzing the business side of law, assessment of attorney search skills, trends in use of reference materials, and much more.

THE SURVEY OF ACADEMIC LIBRARIES, 2004 EDITION
Price: $80   MARCH 2004
ISBN: 1-57440-067-3

This new report is based on a detailed survey of academic libraries, focusing on their acquisition and budget & expenditure policies. Includes data on current and planned purchases of information in print formats and electronic formats and explores planned trade-offs between the two. Also gives precise data on spending on books, e-books, databases, CD-ROMs, journals and other information vehicles. Breaks down electronic information spending into three categories: from aggregators, from publishers directly by subscription, and from publishers, non-subscription. Also presents detailed data on use of document-delivery services, articles 'pulled down' from publisher websites, use of subscription agents, trends in information-literacy training, use of virtual-reference services, extent of library website evaluations, and trends in librarian hiring and salaries. Also examines the perceived attitudes of college administrations towards the library and charts plans for library expansion/contraction.

LICENSING AND COPYRIGHT MANAGEMENT: BEST PRACTICES OF COLLEGE, SPECIAL, AND RESEARCH LIBRARIES
PRICE: $80   MAY 2004
ISBN: 1-57440-068-1

This report looks closely at the licensing and copyright-management strategies of a sample of leading research, college and special libraries and consortiums and includes interviews with leading experts. The focus is on electronic-database licensing, and includes discussions of the most pressing issues: development of consortiums and group buying initiatives, terms of access, liability for infringement, archiving, training and development, free-trial periods, contract language, contract-management software and time-management issues, acquiring and using usage statistics, elimination of duplication, enhancement of bargaining power, open-access publishing policies, interruption-of-service contingency arrangements, changes in pricing over the life of the contract, interlibrary loan of electronic files, copyright clearance, negotiating tactics, uses of consortiums, and many other issues. The report profiles the emergence of consortiums and group-buying arrangements.

CREATING THE DIGITAL ACADEMIC LIBRARY:
Price: $69.50   JULY 2004
ISBN: 1-57440- 071-1

This report looks closely at the efforts of more than ten major academic libraries to develop their digital assets and deal with problems in the area of librarian time management, database selection, vendor relations, contract negotiation and tracking, electronic-resources funding and marketing, technical development, archival access, open access publishing agit prop, use of e-books, digitization of audio and image collections and other areas of the development of the digital academic library. Includes profiles of Columbia University School of Medicine, the Health Sciences Complex of the University of Texas, Duke University Law Library, the University of Indiana Law Library, the University of South Carolina, the University of Idaho, and many others.